THE SILENCE

THE SILENCE

by Lily Gluck Lerner
with SANDRA LEE STUART

LYLE STUART INC.   SECAUCUS, N.J.

Queries regarding rights and permissions
should be addressed to Lyle Stuart Inc.
120 Enterprise Ave., Secaucus, N. J. 07094

Published by Lyle Stuart Inc.
Published simultaneously in Canada
by General Publishing Co. Limited
Don Mills, Ontario

Manufactured in the United States of America

Library of Congress Cataloging in Publication Data

Lerner, Lily Gluck.
    The silence.

    1. Jews in Hungary—Persecutions. 2. Holocaust,
Jewish (1939-1945)—Hungary—personal narratives.
3. Lerner, Lily Gluck. 4. Hungary—Ethnic rela-
tions. I. Stuart, Sandra Lee, joint author.
II. Title.
DS135.H9L43   943.9'004924 [B]   80-20330
ISBN 0-8184-0306-3

With love I dedicate this book to my father.

My mother, Kornell Roth Gluck.

MEMORIAL

This book is a memorial to my beloved mother and my younger brother Ernoke, who at the age of fourteen was gassed in Auschwitz and had no chance to leave an imprint of his visage nor a trace of his existence on this earth.

Like all the others, hatred killed them.
Let love preserve their memory.

ACKNOWLEDGMENTS

There are so many I wish to thank. Among them are:

My sister Margaret, whose love, hope, and mental support have given me the stamina to go on.

Bella Gross, New York City, for the pictures of my grandparents and family.

Eichler Lajos, Tel Aviv, for the list of fifty-two towns forced into the ghetto and for the pictures of the Tolcsva synagogue and of my class.

My dear husband, without whose cooperation this book would not have been possible.

Jerry Jacobs.

And special thanks to Sandra Lee Stuart.

Lily Gluck Lerner
Asheville, N. C.
May 22, 1980

THE SILENCE

To the and the
library and the Lenoir
student of wishes
Rhyne College' best wishes
With my own Lenoir,
Lily

1

Tolcsva, Hungary.

Don't look for it on the map. It exists in relation to other places. More than one hundred kilometers northeast of Budapest. About thirty kilometers from Sátoraljaújhely, which was once county capital of Zemplén. Three kilometers and over the hill from the railway station.

Even today it's a place that would evoke "quaints" and "picturesques" from worldly outsiders wandering in, with its children at holidays dressing in red, white, and green national costumes—dirndls, vests, ribbons, caps, and aprons—and its steeples rising pure and clean over the spread-out village, embosomed in the Tokay-Hegyalya mountain range.

It was, as my father said, a place to live and die.

I was born in Tolcsva fifty-one years ago, daughter of Kornell and Zoltan Gluck, winemakers, store owners, and Jews.

Tolcsva was "picturesque" then, though I never thought of it as such. To me it was crisp springs bringing rains to muddy the unpaved streets. It was skating on the tiny Patak River during subzero winters. It was grape harvests in the fall. It was marveling at the itinerant wine pressers stamping out juice with their bare feet, and my mother, my *anyuka*, preparing goose liver and fresh bread for our lunch in the vineyard. It was long, contemplative walks with my father, my *apuka*, discussing the only time he had been away from Tolcsva, when he fought in the Great War.

It was my sister Margaret. My brothers, Icu and Ernoke. My uncles Samu, Henrich, Lajos, Bernath. Their children, Jossie, Majsi, Magda, Aggi, Rozsi. My beloved Uncle Zsiga, who waited so long to marry. And all the others.

There were so many then, and there are so few now.

Dead: Anyuka. Apuka. My brother Ernoke. My cousin Icu. Magda. Uncle Bernath's wife, Ilonka. Their children Icu and Manyi. Rozsi. Uncle Zsiga and Aunt Helen. Their babies. Aunt Hani and seven of her children. Eszti, Bertha, Benci. Uncle Lajos from Tokay. Cousin Hugo. Szeren. Aunt Zseni, Mother's sister who returned from America to retire in her home country of Hungary. Her husband, Jeno. Jozsi and Herminka and their Bertha and Jossie. Henrich and Helènke. Their son Icu. Samu, my rabbi uncle; his wife, Ethel; and their son, Jossie. My school friend Editt, whose picture I still have. So many of them destroyed in that unnatural disaster of Adolf Hitler's creation.

Human beings couldn't do those things to each other. Yet they did. The nightmare was too awful to be real. Yet it was.

2

I survive. Not because of any miracles, for as I learned quickly in the camps, there are no miracles. I survive because of pure luck. For fourteen million, there was no luck, pure or otherwise. They were erased because they were Jew or Gypsy or of the wrong politics or nationality. They were erased, many as if they had never existed. The Nazis didn't bother keeping lists of their Jewish victims; they kept only body counts.

I don't know what happened to the bodies of Anyuka and brother Ernoke. I can only guess that they were reduced to ashes in Auschwitz's crematoriums and scattered like so much waste. There are no records of Anyuka or Ernoke, no monuments to them; nothing bears their names. They have gone from earth completely.

They, and those like them, both Jew and Gentile, are why I force upon myself the torture of remembering.

In a few years there will be no survivors left. Twenty, thirty years from now, all but a few of us who suffered those horrors will be dead.

For some survivors, there is a compulsion to be only with

other survivors, to keep to themselves and their memories. We would all like to forget.

I cannot allow myself that luxury. I have an obligation to Anyuka, Ernoke, and the others who were exterminated, and those yet unborn, to set this on paper. Let those who are untouched read and perhaps feel a little of what I did. Maybe, just maybe, the knowledge of what happened once will keep it from happening again.

Optimism left me thirty-six years ago in Auschwitz; therefore, I'm not so rosy and foolish as to believe that my nightmare can't happen again. But maybe, just maybe, one person reading this might be affected, and that one person might someday be in the position of stopping a similar horror.

Beyond that, for myself, I must leave something with the names of Ernoke and Anyuka on it, even something as frail as the paper this is written on.

3

I trundled uphill carefully holding Apuka's lunch, his favorite, *habart bab*, string beans cooked in sour cream, and yogurt with fresh bread.

It was a seam day between summer and fall, hot but with the suggestion of coolness to come. A little way off I could see two men, carrying heavy canisters on their backs, spraying the grape vines. It wouldn't be long before harvest, a wonderful time of year, and pressing, and then the juice would go into the vats and into the wine cellar, which was where I was headed.

"Apuka!"

He was waiting for me at our cellar door, one of about seven or ten such doors lined up on the hillside.

"Why, Lily, what a surprise! You have brought me lunch!"

What a surprise! I always brought him lunch. Margaret would stay behind to help Anyuka in the kitchen while I scampered off on any errand I could use as an excuse. If there was any place to go, any excuse to leave the house, it was always Lily's hand that shot up first. Papa taking the train on business trip? Of course, Lily, you can go too. No, Lily, you

On my mother's lap, with my father, my brother Icu, and Margaret.

can't go this time, but it's all right to walk Papa to the station when he leaves at four in the morning. Someone to go to the butcher shop? Why, yes, Lily, but hurry.

Even if I wasn't always so eager to get out, going to the wine cellar on such a hot day would have been a refreshing treat.

"Papa, Mama says I must come back right away, but wouldn't it be all right for me to go into the cellars with you?"

"Well, I do need to check some barrels for leaks, and it would be nice to have someone hold the candle for me. . . ."

No matter how old I got, there was something eerie and fun about the cellar. After each step it was colder and darker, and there were twenty-five steps. You had to have a candle. There was no other way to see once you reached the bottom, although I always wondered if Papa really needed one. He knew exactly which year each of the one hundred or two hundred vats was and what quality wine it held.

He could walk down one of the aisles, point to a barrel up on the long log rails, and say, "1914," without even looking. Some of those barrels were mossy with age, having been rolled in when my father's father had owned the vineyard. I don't know, but there might have been vats from his father's father's father.

Tolcsva was in a renowned wine-growing region, although nearby Tokay really had the worldwide reputation. Jews had been wine growers in the region since the eighteenth century. In 1723 seven Jewish families, probably from Poland, received permission from the landowners of the surrounding area to settle and to lease the vineyards. By 1724, twenty-four Jewish families were living in Tolcsva; 1735, forty-three; and 1771, fifty-four. By the time I was thirteen, in 1941, out of some 1,000 residents, 363 were Jewish.

My parents were not rich, by any standards. They were middle-class, working hard to have what they did. Besides the fifteen acres of grapes, we had a few acres for wheat, a little more for vegetables and cattle feed, a couple of cows, our wine cellar, and a small shoe shop. There was a girl who helped out my mother, and during harvesttime, Szalancy, our caretaker, hired on as many as fifteen people.

And I was happy, and loved, and life seemed almost perfect in Tolcsva.

Memories, specially those from childhood, do not form linear progressions. Times and years, ages and dates are afterthoughts, tacked on when asked, "When did that happen?" What I remember is a collage of incidents and events, feelings

Father, at left, and Szalancy, the caretaker, showing the vineyards to Ruth Gross, Jossi Gluck, Joe Gross, and an unidentified man.

and friends, jumbled on to each other without much pattern but with a lot of texture.

"Is it done, Mr. Wrubel? Is it done?"

"Now, Lily, how could it possibly be done? Your mother just brought the cloth in to me the other day, and you haven't even had a fitting yet."

It was Passover time, which meant that Margaret and I would get our new dress for the year. Mama would go into Sátoraljaújhely (or, once in a long while, even Budapest) and select cloth.

I was always excited about a new dress, but this year—I must have been nine or ten—Mama had bought the most wonderful fabric. It was linen-like and beige, sprinkled with blue racquets and red tennis balls. Mr. Wrubel was going to sew little pockets on the left and three pleats on either side. Margaret and I—we always got the identical dresses, even though we weren't twins—were going to make all the other girls at school absolutely jealous. Not that we would be wearing the dresses at school for a good long while. That would wait for at least another year, till another new dress was made.

Store-bought dresses were a rarity in a small town like Tolcsva, so Mr. Wrubel was always stitching. Passover dresses for the Jewish girls, Easter clothes for the Gentiles. Once in a while, Mr. Schwartz, the tailor, would make a suit for a man. (Men prolonged the lives of their suits by having them turned inside out after a few years of wear. Mr. Schwartz would carefully pull the suit apart and put it back together with the wrong side out.

As in the rest of Hungary, most of Tolcsva's middle class was Jewish, although there were poor Jews as well. There was Green the baker, whose shop had the most enormous ovens. My friends and I would stand forever watching dough rise and rolls brown. And the smell! If nothing else could make you salivate, that smell could.

There was Klein, the ironmonger. A leaking pot and I was off to Klein's tiny store, two steps down. He would take one round piece of metal, stick it on the outside of the pot, another round piece on the inside, and rivet them together.

Two of the butchers were Jewish, and another Jew owned the slaughterhouse. The only car in town, chauffeur driven, no less, was owned by Adonyi Pista, the lawyer, who owned a good deal of land and was very occupied with all manner of legal and civic affairs. I used to wonder as the car whizzed by what it was like to sit in the back, bumping along, with all the children staring at you, wanting to be you.

Adonyi Pista had both Jewish and Gentile clients, since he was the only lawyer in Tolcsva. When it came to commerce and business, there really wasn't any segregation. Jews didn't go only to Jewish stores. Everyone knew everyone and shopped wherever they wanted.

And there was Doctor Klein, a general practitioner, about my father's age, who took care of everyone in Tolcsva and the surrounding areas. He always seemed to be bundling off in his buggy to tend to someone or other. But I suppose, being a bachelor, his entire life was his medicine. Such a lovely person.

I went to Doctor Klein's office, which was in his house, by myself. I didn't even tell Anyuka, I suppose because I had acute pre-teenage embarrassment.

I was worried. I needed a respected medical opinion.

"Of course, Lily, you may come in." I never had any doubt that Doctor Klein would see me.

"Are you sick?" asked the doctor with the same tone and concern he would have had if Apuka or Anyuka had summoned him.

"Doctor Klein, it's something that Icu said. I've got to know if it's true." Icu was seven years older than I was, and what he said always made such sense. Maybe I was doomed to deformity.

"Lily, you certainly look sick. Tell me exactly what Icu said."

"He told me to come see you because . . . he said I had to see you because . . . because I have bad posture and I'm going to be a hunchback. Will you examine me, Doctor Klein, to see if I'm going to be a hunchback?"

Doctor Klein looked very grave, and I prepared myself for the worst.

"I don't have to examine you. I can tell you now that you won't be a huchback. But you will have to do one thing— you will have to straighten up."

I knew Doctor Klein would have the answer! After all, he had already saved my life once.

It was wash day, in the dead of winter, and it was cold. Erzsi, the girl who worked for Anyuka, had helped her take down the curtains and strip the beds, which amounted to so much laundry that it couldn't fit in our wooden wash tub. The only place large enough to rinse everything was the river.

The air was frigid, and the water was even worse. We worked quickly. We were almost done and ready to head back to the warmth of the kitchen stove, when a puff of wind caught a handkerchief and lifted it away. Possessions were few and dear; even a handkerchief was precious.

Erzsi panicked. "Quick, Lily!" she screamed. "Grab it before it blows away!"

The handkerchief had already landed, in the water. I was not one to ponder and contemplate. If Erzsi said grab the handkerchief, I grabbed the handkerchief, even if it meant splashing into the near-freezing water, shoes and all.

I got pneumonia.

Pneumonia, in Hungary in the thirties, was often fatal and probably would have been in my case, except for Doctor Klein.

He came quickly when my condition worsened. He gave me an injection of something and made sure that Anyuka knew to keep ice-cold compresses on my forehead and chest to bring down the fever. He kept vigil when it was needed and checked up on me often when it wasn't.

The road from the railroad station, although unpaved, was hardened from countless feet and wagon wheels packing it down over the years.

On either side of it were fields planted with grain or feed for animals. At some times of year red and blue flowers would blow and bend in the wind. At other times the fields waved and waved in acres of uniform green. There were four-leaf clovers and bouquets of lilacs to be picked.

All these fields belonged to Baron Waldbot Kelemen, a member of parliament, who was one of the largest landowners in the area. The two neat rows of white stucco houses were for his many workers. I always watched those houses carefully when I walked by. For some reason, storks liked to nest on their red ceramic roofs, maybe because of all the open

Aunt Hani, left, on a visit to Grandmother Gluck in
Tolcsva. The European women wore scarves; Americanized Hani did not.

fields nearby where they could spread their wings and soar.

I was on the alert walking by because you never knew when a stork would fly off toward Tolcsva. If it did, and if it landed on a village rooftop, that meant, as all the children would tell you, a baby would be making a squalling appearance soon in that house. It was good to be the one to see the stork. It gave you special knowledge no one else had.

Apuka received another letter from Uncle Samu, and Anyuka wasn't happy. For that matter, Apuka wasn't overjoyed either.

Samu was one of Apuka's older brothers. By today's standards, his was a large family, with six boys and one girl. Hani, the eldest, had emigrated to the United States when she was sixteen. Just upped and moved, looking for a better life. She found it too, with her husband, a man named Gross, running a jewelry store together when they were married, running it herself when they divorced. As a child, I never met Aunt Hani, not being born when she and her children, Ruth, Bella (nicknamed Peszi), and Joseph, visited in the early 1920s. I didn't see many of our relatives, because distances, even short ones, were so difficult to traverse then.

Uncle Jozsi and Aunt Herminka lived in Szepsi. It couldn't have been more than ninety-five kilometers from Tolcsva. Still, I rarely saw them. First because Szepsi was under Czechoslovakian occupation, which made visits almost impossible. But then, even after the border was moved and Szepsi was again under the Hungarian flag, ninety-five kilometers, as short as it might seem, was too far for casual visiting.

I do remember when one of their daughters, Luci, came one summer. People often visited relatives in Tolcsva during the summer. It was cooler there than in the cities, and also had therapeutic waters. What was Luci when she came, nineteen? And I was twelve. She was so grown-up, so well dressed. I looked at her all the time in all those beautiful dresses. Uncle Jozsi was in the yard-goods business and seemed very well off, from everything I had heard. I was so happy that Luci had come to visit. That one time was the only time I met her. Once, and that was all.

Apuka had two other brothers who lived in Tokay. One, Henrich, was married to Helènke. They had three sons, Majsi, Icu, and Tibi, and one daughter, Bertha. The other brother was Lajos. He and his wife, Boriska, had six children—three daughters, Rozsi, Irene, and Kato, and three sons, Imre, Miklos, and Hugo.

The youngest of my father's brothers was Zsiga, who resolutely remained a bachelor, although Apuka engaged in numerous matchmaking attempts, trying to marry him off.

Zsiga was a salesman, always making enough for his modest needs but not much more. He was very introverted and blamed his experience in World War I for that. Introverted or not, he still wasn't going to be pushed into marrying anyone, no matter how many times Apuka said to someone, "I have a brother. I'd like to see him settled down." No matter how many times the friends would come up with likely candidates and Apuka would go to the family to see if a match could be arranged. Zsiga always managed to find a way to extricate himself just short of the *chuppa*, the ceremonial canopy under which Jews get married. When Zsiga finally did marry, he was in his forties, and it was to a woman he had found himself.

Besides Zsiga, who lived in Tolcsva, Uncle Samu was part of the family I did see a lot. Samu was a rabbi who also lived in Tolcsva for many years with his stern-faced wife, Ethel, and their ever-so-studious son, Jossie. Not until I was a teenager did Samu move to Tornaalya, to be a rabbi there.

Then the letters started arriving.

It was always money.

"I have to pay my dues," Uncle Samu would write. Or "I have to pay my taxes. You better send me some money."

Apuka would grumble; yet he always sent whatever sum Samu demanded. It was if Samu expected help, even though he was Apuka's older brother. My father had remained in Tolcsva with the vineyards. When he married Anyuka, there was never any question that he would move to her village of Olaszliska, although it was only five kilometers away. Tolcsva was his home, the place he intended to live and die. And the vineyards, the growing, the harvesting, the wine were all him.

Grandfather had left the vineyards to Apuka. They were

Aunt Ethel and Uncle Samu.

about fifteen acres in all. I'm not sure that deep down Samu didn't resent that, maybe a little bit. Apuka seemed to have got more, and Samu had been "punished" in a strange sort of way because he was a rabbi. So Samu was forever short of money for dues and taxes and such, and Apuka seemed comparatively well off, with the land, vineyards, and shoe store. Hence the special-delivery letters, more demands than entreaties.

I didn't hear Anyuka complain about the letters; only Apuka complained. Relations between her and Ethel had never been the best.

When Anyuka and Apuka were first married they lived in Grandparents Glucks' house in Tolcsva. Ethel and Samu also shared the houses. There were two, besides the stable. It became a question of sisters-in-law being too close for amicability. Ethel, so sharp-tongued and over-conscious of

Left to right: Jossi Gluck, Ethel, my mother, Hani, Grandma Gluck, my brother Icu, my father, and Ruth Gross (kneeling).

her awkward limp. Anyuka, with her broad-faced beauty, would have been the belle of the ball in a society that had such things. When such a lovely addition came into the family, Anyuka naturally became the center of attention. Ethel must have hated it.

"Anyuka! Anyuka!" I was so excited, I couldn't wait to get through the gate before shouting across the yard to the kitchen.

"Anyuka! I'm going to be in a community play! Isn't it wonderful?"

Anyuka was kneading dough that would go to Green's to be baked and then come back golden and fresh for our table.

"That's so nice, Lily. And what will you be playing?"

Why did she have to ask that? I didn't think Anyuka would object to my role, but I was uneasy.

"Anyuka, you know how I'm taller than the rest of the girls. And you know there are more girls than boys in school. Well, we're going to have very nice costumes. And I will be very good in my part."

"I'm sure you will be, but what will you be playing?"

There was no way of keeping it from her. After all, it was a small town, and she would come to the play.

"I'm going to play a boy."

"A boy? You'll have to be a very good actress, because you're much too pretty to be a boy."

"I knew you wouldn't be angry."

"Why should I? If your teacher wants you to be a boy, so be it."

"But Anyuka, what will Uncle Samu and Aunt Ethel do if they find out?"

That was the nub of the problem. Uncle Samu and Aunt

Ethel. I could picture them, in outrage, storming the stage and pulling me off by the scruff of my neck. It wasn't becoming, proper, I knew they would say, for a nice religious girl to be going around so outrageously dressed.

Anyuka was smiling. "Maybe they'll never find out."

They never did.

In Tolcsva there were three elementary schools. The largest, not surprisingly, was Roman Catholic—not surprisingly since 70 percent of Hungary was Catholic, the next largest religious group being Calvinist.

Ours was a one-room school, the kind that today, in 1980, is all of a sudden enjoying a new respect. We had one teacher, Mr. Lukacs, teaching all six grades. There couldn't have been more than fifty or fifty-five students in the entire school.

The second grade of the Jewish elementary school in Tolcsva. I am circled.

Although a Jewish school, it was government supported, and the sign outside the door so stated.

We crammed a tremendous amount of learning into those 8:00 A.M. to 2:30 P.M. school days—geography, history, mathemattics. When final examinations came in June, and the county examiner arrived, we all trooped into school in our best outfits and with bouquets of flowers to lay on Mr. Lukacs's desk.

Parents came also, lining the wall, to listen to our poetry recitals.

Like much of my childhood, I enjoyed school tremendously. I read the books in our minuscule library and got straight A's.

Of course, being the rough and tumble I was, I really liked our physical-fitness program. Running, long jumping, rope jumping, and the simple drill maneuvers, raising, lowering, brandishing the red, white, and green Hungarian flag. At the end of the school year the entire school population crammed into horse-drawn buggies, to be taken to a special meet between all the schools in the Huta valley.

I can't remember that we ever took first prize, or second, but the competition and the trip were the reward.

Some of my favorite friends were Zsuzsi, the grocer's daughter, Vera, whose father worked in the bank, Eta, the wagoneer's daughter, and Magda, the fireman's daughter.

Summer's end. First the ripened wheat would be harvested. Several of the men hired by Szalancy would mow it with long-handled sickles. Sheaves were tied with ropes made from wheat stalks, and then crisscrossed into square piles and left in the field to dry.

The end of the fieldwork was signaled by a celebration. A wreath was made by weaving flowers into wheat stalks. Then. forming a procession behind a woman holding on high a wreath, symbol of harvest's end, the peasants would sing their way back to the village.

But the work was not done, of course. Once dried, the *cseplo*, a tall, horse-drawn threshing machine, would arrive. It was owned by a local locksmith, who rented it out to the various farmers. The *cseplo* was driven up and down the rows of wheat sheaves while men with long pitchforks threw the wheat into the machine. Separated from the chaff, seeds poured into sacks tied to openings in the *cseplo*. Depending on how good the crop was, threshing would take two or three days.

Apuka hired a local wagoneer, Zelenak, to take him and the wheat to a mill three kilometers away. The donkeys pulling the cart were so slow that the trip there and back took the entire day.

The decision of how much of different types of flour was to be ground was crucial, for there was no running to the A&P for more "all-white" flour for cakes and bisquits, or "half-white" for white bread, or "brown" for darker bread, or farina for gravy flour, or the waste *corpa* that the cows ate. You had to make your decision in the fall for the entire year.

When Apuka returned with the flour, it was the ritual for him to present it to Anyuka for her inspection and approval. The success of the milling often depended on the miller's mood on that particular day, but nonetheless, Anyuka judged it, discussed it, and then had it stored in separate bins for winter's use.

Fall was, as it has been through the ages, a preparation for winter and the rest of the year until another harvest was brought in.

Our apples had to be stored in a cool place; peaches, apricots, currants, and gooseberries canned or preserved. Purple plums, ripe and shaken from their tree, were collected in enamel kitchen pails that were usually used for drinking water. Neighbor women congregated for a day of almost festive gossiping and plum pitting.

Once cored, the plums went into an enormous brass urn and a hired woman stirred the mixture over a log fire all day long, until the thickened preserves were done.

It was fun sneaking a taste from the plum mix, but everyone got a taste after the preserves were transferred into wooden boxes lined with thick paper. Then it was a party of licking the inside of the urn before it was washed and carried to the house of someone else who rented it from us by the day.

And fall meant *szuret*, the harvest of the grapes, one of the last fruits to be picked. Szuret was close to a miracle for the winegrower. From planting to harvest he waited and worried. If rain was followed too closely by too much sun, leaves might be scorched unless sprayed at once. He worried over hail, over too much sun, too little, over too much rain, too little. Planting to harvest was torment. Szuret meant the torment ended—until spring's work began the cycle again.

During the growing, workers tied the vines at least three times, sprayed when necessary, and set traps for pesty rabbits. At harvest they came, each selecting a row of vines, to cut the grape bunches and drop them into pails. A young boy carried these to large barrels that were transported to our house.

I used to ride on the barrel wagon. It was my job to see that no mischievous children filched any of the grapes. All

day the wagon carried the barrels. All day the men picked—
except for lunchtime. Then the men roasted squares of pork
over bonfires. Although the goose liver Anyuka prepared for
us was delicious, I looked enviously upon that heavenly-
smelling, forbidden pork the others were eating.

Pressing took place at our warehouse. A strong fellow
would climb barefooted into one of the three-legged vats,
put some of the grapes into a burlap bag, and get as much
juice as he could by pressing the bag against the side of the
vat. The crushed remains still in the bag would be transferred
to another, larger vat, where two other men, with their
shoes on, would stamp out even more juice.

A different kind of wine was gotten from each step of the
pressing. Nothing was wasted, the very dregs, the *torko*, were
left outside for a couple of weeks and then taken to a brewery
to be made into *torko palinka*, a drink similar to brandy.

The grape harvest had its celebration, with a wreath even
more beautiful than that of the wheat harvest.

Our gate was opened in the morning so that Dudas, the
shepherd, and his two diligent little dogs could herd our
cows to pasture. He also tended a couple of bulls someone
else owned and would be sure to tell Father when a mating
occurred.

It was a great day when a calf arrived, after months of
gestation. The wiggling little things are cute when they are
born, but the cuteness quickly gives way to cowness. I'd
closely watch as Cifra, our best milker, licked clean every
part of her calves. Only the females were kept. The butcher
fetched the male calves once they were big enough for
slaughter. We children always managed to find something
very important to do away from home when that day arrived.

33

When winter's frigidness (it was sometimes ten or fifteen degrees below zero) kept the cows in the stable, they were fed hay, sugar, beets, and dried cornstalks three times a day, starting at four in the morning. We all knew how to tend the livestock and keep the stable clean. And we also knew the importance of keeping a close watch on the cows as they drank water from the pail. Cows are not bright animals. You'd have to pick their heads up by the horns between gulps; otherwise they'd drink too fast and get sick. When that happened Apuka had to massage their backs and squeeze soda water down their throats to make them burp. Neither Apuka nor Anyuka would leave the stable until the ailing cow was better.

Mrs. Rhinehart was sitting on her sofa when I paid one of my after-school visits. She was our next door neighbor, when I was very young, before we moved into my grand-parents' house. I was quite sure that Mrs. Rhinehart was at least a hundred years old.

Her small, fragile body, swaddled in several skirts, was bent in concentration over the piece of white cloth she was working on. Deliberately, meticulously, she executed stitch after stitch, each one perfect, but each one receiving a squinting examination. Mrs. Rhinehart was never one to rush her sewing, and yet this was very different.

"What's that you're working on?" Who needed salutations or invitations? I plopped down beside her.

Not even glancing up, Mrs. Rhinehart said, "Never mind— just thread that other needle for me."

Stitch after stitch. Her solemnity was making me squirm and fiddle, but she continued to ignore me.

I couldn't stand it any longer. "Please, Mrs. Rhinehart. What are you sewing?"

Finally she paused, for the tiniest of seconds. "It's the dress I am going to meet God in. I'm sewing my *tehrihan*."

I had been to funerals. Mother took me, saying the greatest *mitzvah*, the greatest respect, one can give is to accompany a dead person to burial, because that person can never repay you.

It was so sad to see the men carrying a casket to the cemetery, followed by the surviving family and practically every other Jew from the village.

Although I had been to many funerals, I had never actually seen a dead body. I tried to imagine what Mrs. Rhinehart would be like, not breathing, lying perfectly still in the darkness of her casket. And then I thought of that first time I had walked in a funeral procession, tightly holding Anyuka's hand. I had looked up at her, studying her face, watching every movement of her eyes and mouth, the motion of the few wisps of hair that escaped her scarf, and I tried to imagine her perfectly still.

No, I had thought. *My parents can never die. I could never accept losing them. How do other people live after their parents have gone?*

Anyuka had almost died in the worldwide flu epidemic that lasted from 1917 to 1919, killing twenty to thirty million people, the twentieth century's version of the black plague.

At her sickest, when it looked as if she wouldn't make it, Anyuka made a vow to God. She promised that if she survived, once she married she would cut her hair and keep her head covered with a scarf, and if she had a son, she would raise him learning the Torah.

Anyuka didn't have to keep her promise until June 20, 1920, when, at the age of twenty-two, she married the twenty-seven-year-old Zoltan Gluck. It must have been a tremendous jolt and readjustment leaving her parents, Majsi and Szeren Roth, her large family, and the place she had lived her entire life.

Anyuka was one of the last of her brothers and sisters to leave the nest. One brother, Erno, a brilliant boy who had made the quota of Jews to be accepted into medical school, had died there. Anyuka never discussed any details, so something always seemed mysterious about his death.

Her other brother, Bernath, had married a woman named Ilona, and they had two children, Margaret, or Manyi, as she was called, and Icu.

Anyuka's oldest sister, Hani, had married quite young and immediately started having children. She didn't stop until there were twelve.

Her sister Esther married Benci and had two daughters. One was poisoned on her wedding night by her own groom. Sister Szeren married Majsi, had a daughter, Berthus, and then was divorced. It fell to Anyuka, young as she was at the time, to virtually raise Berthus, which she did until a mutual friend told Zoltan that he knew a wonderful unmarried girl in Olaszliska and then told Kornell that he knew a commendable single fellow in Tolcsva, and wasn't it wonderful the two villages were only five miles apart?

They were married one year before Icu put in his appearance in 1921. Margaret was the next arrival, in 1926. Then came me in 1928 and beautiful little Ernoke in 1930. (Ernoke had such a sweet face and wonderfully golden curls that he would often be mistaken for a girl. "No, no!" I would scream indignantly, running to the defense of his gender. "He's a boy! See—a boy!" And I would pull up his baby gown to exhibit the proof.)

As with Apuka's side of the family, we didn't see much of Anyuka's relatives, although once a year we would make the trip to Grandfather's grave. And sometimes then I would see my cousins and think how lucky I was that such wonderful people were a part of me and always would be.

When I'm older, I would think, *I will see them as much as I want*. It was a pleasant, comforting thought.

So beautiful, so peaceful—Tolcsva seems so far away.

4

The peace, the beauty, was, of course, all a veneer. Brushed on lightly, to a myopic eye it might have been good enough to pass for the real things. But it was always a veneer. Someone more sophisticated and wiser would have noticed the ugliness visible where the surface was scratched. I was neither.

What did it matter to me that there were no Jews in Tolcsva's government? Government to me was the hated mayor, Szalai, who, as far as I was concerned, had always been in office. Father used to complain of Szalai's high-handed and unfeeling way of dealing with tax delinquents. Miss one payment, and Szalai's men were at your door to collecting an "in lieu of," a bedroom set or a table or anything else of any kind of value. The man was completely devoid of sympathy or compassion. But he was a fixture as was his lackey, Szotak, who swept the town hall and was the town crier, going through the street shouting that so-and-so's house had burned, that tax time had come, or whatever. He and Szalai were the system, and the system did not include Jews.

The gentile children would yell, *"Jew! Jew!"* at us sometimes on our way to school. But it didn't bother me that much. We were Jews, after all. Snowballs with rock centers

Uncle Samu and Jossie.

that flew over our schoolyard fence from the Roman Catholic side were merely bad kids tormenting good.

If there had always been, for as long as you had been alive, a quota for Jews attending the universities, that was how life was. You accepted it. Maybe in a place like the United States, things were different. But you lived in Hungary, and despite these things life to me was awfully good. Why, hadn't Admiral Miklos Horthy, the regent of Hungary, a country that had become a kingdom without a king—hadn't he once sipped my Apuka's wine at the annual tasting in Budapest?

The one evidence of anti-Semitism I couldn't overlook or deny was the treatment of cousin Jossie, Uncle Samu's son.

Jossie was a very religious boy and very studious. He was always immersed in books, more pouring himself into them than poring over them. There wasn't enough for him to read and learn. Using nothing but dictionaries, he taught himself several languages. And there was religion. It was his life and his meaning.

Spindly, frail, cautious, he had the complexion of one who rarely stepped into sunlight. About the only time Jossie left his house was to hurry along to temple.

Wearing his traditional long, black garb, head bowed, eyes almost shut so that he wouldn't accidentally look upon the face of a woman, Jossie was an obvious target for malicious little and not so little tormentors. Some of the meaner kids waited on the streets for him, to heckle and jeer, to pull his coat and shove him. It was never enough to actually injure him, but it was more than enough to make him suffer.

"How do they always know when I'm coming?" he'd sigh. "Why do they do it?"

He never fought back. Aunt Ethel would boast after these

attacks, "I brought my son up to behave with honor to his fellowman. He was taught to respect others. If anyone hits him with a rock, he has been told hit back with bread. I am proud of him."

He never hit back. The most he would do was jerk away his coat and move on without a word or whimper of protest.

I could never understand what they wanted from Jossie either. He was odd because he studied so much and had his long blond locks. But I studied too—I liked to read Sinclair Lewis and the other books in our school library. Of course, I also liked to get out and do many things. Still, I could see no reason for them to torture Jossie as they did.

I would get so mad when it happened. Why didn't Jossie hit back? Why didn't he yell and scream and kick at them? Why I would have. But even Anyuka said you never hit back.

5

Hungary's has been a convulsive history of conquering and being conquered, of feudal landowners jealously undermining weak and strong monarchs, of religious tensions between Christian and pagan, Catholic and Protestant. It is a history of a fierce, proud majority being ruled but never subjugated by one foreign power after another. It is a history of buffering the east from the west and vice versa, of amalgamating and aassimilating other cultures but never completely dissolving the parts into the whole. What was to happen to Hungary and its Jews in the twentieth century was the product of the ten preceding centuries.

The Hungarian majority was and is the Magyars, a nomadic, fighting people who came west to the Carpathian Basin from the Ural Mountains in the ninth century. They were one of the many warring hordes to sweep over Europe after the fall of the Roman Empire. Although from the east, with their own peculiar Finno-Ugric language and their own brand of paganism, the Magyars moved inexorably through history toward the west and westernization.

Initially there were seven separate Magyar tribes that banded together under one elected chieftain, Arpad, to conquer the Slavs and others who had the misfortune of living in the Danube Valley when the Magyars moved into the neighborhood.

Although the Danube was theirs, the Magyars used it primarily as a refueling base for their marauding and pillaging, which streteched from the boot of Italy to the Pyrennes and from Constantinople to the North Sea.

The raids went on for decades. Finally, in retaliation, the Holy Roman Empire amassed a military force of its own and effectively put an end to the Magyar marauding at the battle of Augsburg.

The trouncing by the Holy Roman Empire not only put an end to the raids, but it also underscored the Magyars' need to align themselves with some power, caught and pinched as they were between the eastern and western forms of Christianity. With that in mind, Prince Geza, the great grandson of Arpad, whose descendants had kept getting elected as head of the tribe, chose to throw in the Hungarian lot with the west. Geza had his son Stephen baptized a Roman Catholic. On taking the throne and marrying a Bavarian princess, Stephen set about converting the rest of his country, thereby earning himself sainthood. Hence he is now known as Saint Stephen.

Stephen was a strong monarch. Hungary wasn't to have many of those as the landowning aristocracy constantly pushed the country deeper and deeper into feudalism, a system that gave them more power.

In 1222, something called the Golden Bull, a distant cousin to England's Magna Carta, was forced upon the king, limiting his power even further. One apparently unforeseen effect of the Golden Bull was that it completely disenfranchised the peasant, a condition that remained for centuries. (In 1514 the peasants rebelled. After much bloodshed, the rebellion was quelled, and the peasants were thrown into virtual slavery for the next two hundred years.)

The first, but not the last, time the Magyars had reason to regret throwing in with the West was in 1241, when the

Mongols tried to go through Hungary on their way to overrun Europe. The Hungarians fought back, and for the next year, with no assistatnce from any European neighbor, they held off the Mongols, suffering much devastation.

Finally the Mongols moved back to the Russian steppes. They offered the Hungarians a chance to reconsider their allegiance and ally themselves with the Mongols. But the Magyars had chosen west over east and, for better or worse, were determined to stick to that decision.

The Mongolian threat was soon supplanted by a Turkish one. Thanks to acquisitions and annexations, Hungarian lands included vast territories, even stretching down the Black Sea to Turkey. When Turkey wanted to expand north, Hungary was in the way. So the Turks pushed and encroached, a little here, a bit there, wherever possible. It took a brilliant Hungarian tactician, Janos Hunyadi, to push the Turks back, defeating them at Belgrade in 1456. Hunyadi's son Magyas (also known as Corvinius Matthias) managed to annex Bohemia, Silessia, Moravia, and lower Austria. Unfortunately, his death precipitated a period of feudal anarchy.

The Hunyadis, strong leaders that they were, had been able to hold off further Turkish attempts at expansion. With a strong leader, the Hungarians had a chance against the Turks. Without one, it was all over.

In 1526, defeated at the Battle of Mohacs, Hungary fell to Turkey and was promptly carved and partitioned. The bulk went to the victor. Transylvania, a territory that was the least assimilated into the Hungarian whole, was allowed to be ruled by its own princes under Turkish suzerainty. The west and north were handed over to the Hapsburgs, Austria's royal family, who had long been jockeying covetously toward Hungary. It was easier for the Turks to appease the Hapsburgs than to battle them.

So it remained for an oppressive century and a half, until the

Turks were driven out, not by Hungarian liberators, but by the Hapsburgs. The Austrians tired of having only a paltry piece; now they wanted the whole pie.

If the Magyars had hoped for better treatment from the Hapsburgs than the Turks, they were in for a bitter surprise. Only Transylvania, playing Machiavellian games, was able to remain relatively independent by continuing to work the Turks against the Austrians.

The feudal system, by its very nature, impeded any drive for Hungarian independence, fostering splinter groups and rivalries. There was so much internal bickering that no united front could be formed. That's not to say there were no stabs made at getting rid of the Austrian yoke. There were many—so many that in the 1700s the Austrians encouraged and fostered immigration to Hungary by more peaceable peoples than the Magyars, hoping these peoples would be easier to keep in line.

In 1848, however, there was one major push for independence. The Hungarians by then felt strong enough to begin making demands, such as establishing a Hungarian government in Hungary, not Austria; having an elected legislature; being taxed uniformly; having freedom of the press; and reestablishing Transylvania as part of Hungary.

The Hapsburg king in Hungary actually went along with the demands. This did not sit well in Vienna; therefore, the king didn't sit much longer in Budapest. The new king promptly rescinded all promises made by his predecessor and had to call in Austrian and Russian troops in response to the unrest that followed. So ended the revolution of 1848.

As punishment, Hungary became an annexed, poor-relation part of Austria for twenty years. In 1867, a compromise was finally reached in which Hungary's status was improved through the creation of a dual monarchy. A common king ruled, with parliaments in both states. Thus was Austria-Hungary born.

It was an excruciating time for Hungarian politicians. They

were in the classic position of being caught in the middle, having to juggle angry citizens at home, who believed their country was getting the short end of the arrangement, and their political counterparts in Austria, who despite the compromise still felt they were the absolute rulers of Hungary.

The compromise was ended by World War I. Hungary did not opt for autonomy and join the Allies. Hungary stuck with Austria, hoping to get more land from the Central Powers if they won than they would get from an alignment with the Allies if they won. It was a big gamble that Hungary lost in a big way.

It wasn't just that the Allies won, and Hungary didn't get new territory. The Treaty of Triano in 1920 hacked off 72 percent of Hungary's prewar land, creating countries out of what had been Hungarian minority peoples. In doing so, the treaty created a whole new set of problems and a new minority: These countries still had Magyars in them, and the treaty made Hungarians the new minority in the new countries.

Hungary had tried to save its territories at war's end by forming a republic under the leadership of Count Mihaly Karolyi, a leftist. His regime lasted only from October 1918 until March 1919, when other leftists combined with communists and forced Karolyi to resign. The leader of the new government was a communist, Bela Kun, whose five months in office have been characterized as a reign of terror. Among Bela Kun's followers were some Jews. In years to come that fact was dredged up repeatedly as an excuse for anti-Semitism.

Bela Kun was defeated by the Romanians, and into the political breach marched Admiral Miklos Horthy, an arch-conservative. The parliament elected Horthy regent of Hungary in 1920, realizing that the Allies would never again allow an Austrian king to rule both countries.

At its beginning, Horthy's regime was also terror filled and and harsh, as he attempted to expunge and punish all remnants of Bela Kun. This included retaliations and pogroms against Jews. However as Horthy's regime settled in, actions against Jews abated.

In a country that had been filled with minorities, Jews were a very important group. They accounted for about 5 percent of the population, but their importance was far greater than the percentage suggests, for Jews made up a major portion of the country's middle class. The aristocratic landowners felt it beneath their dignity and station to indulge in too much business activity. Peasants historically and traditionally were kept to the land, with little upward mobility. It fell, in large part, to the Jews to fill the professional and commercial vacuum. Approximately half of the private doctors, a third of the journalists, half the lawyers, and a third of those involved in trade were Jewish. Pragmatism would seem to dictate some protection of such an important sector of the society.

Then, too, Jews had fought in World War I. National honor demanded fair treatment for its veterans.

Pragmatism gets overruled. National honor gets sullied.

Immediately after World War I, quotas were instituted, setting the number of Jews allowed in universities. Jews were kept out of public office.

The memory of Bela Kun did recede, and desire for scapegoats dimmed, and though many of them emigrated, Jews continued to live in Hungary as they had for generations, in an uneasy peace and suppressed fear.

Adolf Hitler and Hungary's continued expansionist yearnings changed all that. Hungary wanted back what it had lost with the Treaty of Triano. Again, it decided to side with the powers it believed most accommodating to that end. Hungary was sure Hitler was the key to getting the lands returned.

So it was that in 1938, a month after the German dictator annexed Austria, the Hungarian parliament passed its "Jewish law," a law meant to appease Hitler and demonstrate the

Hungarian resolve to further his aims. Not so coincidentally, this law was passed at the same time Hungary was approaching Hitler about Czechoslovakia.

The law of 1938 decreed that a person was Jewish if he or she was so by religion; had left the Jewish community or had converted after July 31, 1919; or had been born after July 31, 1919, of Jewish parents, no matter what his or her present religion was. The quotas allowed Jews to make up 20 percent of any profession and 20 percent of the staffs of private industry, commerce, and banking.

A year later, when Hungary had designs on Romania and Yugoslavia, another Jewish law, far more stringent, was enacted. Under its definition, someone was Jewish by religion; as was anyone who had converted to Christianity on or after her or his seventh birthday; anyone who had converted even before the seventh birthday, if her or his parents had not also converted before January 1, 1939 or whose family had not been in Hungary since 1849.

The new law's occupational quotas covered almost every field of endeavor. Private businesses in industry, commerce, and banking were not allowed to have a staff that was more than 12 percent Jewish. No Jews were allowed to be civil servants or journalists. Jews could hold only 6 percent of all trading licenses and 20 percent of public contracts (and by 1943 that, too, was to be reduced to 6 percent). Agricultural property was taken away and redistributed. Within five years, no Jew was to have a license to sell state-monopoly products.

Jews were to be effectively eliminated from public life and trading.

If that law hadn't been bad enough, another was passed when Hungary joined Germany in declaring war on Russia. It was by far the most complex and harsh in its definition, including as Jews children of half-Jewish mothers whose fathers were unknown if either the child or the mother was not baptized at the time of the former's birth; persons with two Jewish grandparents married to some with one Jewish grandparents; and so on.

In 1941, when this last law came into being, there were 725,000 Jews in Hungary. Another 62,000 *became* "Jewish" by this law.

The Catholic church had fought against elements of the definition, though not out of any altruism toward Jews. Rather, it had attempted to protect its converts. It lost that fight with the 1941 law.

Aryanization had begun in 1939, but the Germans weren't satisfied with its pace. By 1943 Jews had been completely eliminated from the trades dealing with textiles, rags, church articles, cement, onions, wine, eggs, milk, fats, hogs, and cattle. They were no longer allowed to export potatoes, fruit, hay or straw. They could no longer wholesale sugar, gasoline, fodder, coal, leather, or milk. They were out of the restaurant business.

Ironically, Germany suffered from Hungarian Aryanization. German businessmen complained that their imports from Hungary had fallen off because of the incredible inefficiency of the new Hungarian trade-license holders. It was estimated that of the fifteen hundred trade textile licenses given out after Jews were removed from the trade, the holders of only thirty could be trusted enough to be given credit. (A good number of prostitutes were among those who had received licenses.)

In his book *The Destruction of the European Jews*, Raul Hilberg told of a report from one German textile executive on the problem.

> The executive . . . was in the textile business, and he was acutely interested in changes taking place in the Hungarian textile sector. He concluded quickly that there was no comparison between the Aryanization in Germany and Hungary. For the implementation of Aryanization, he said, the Hun-

garians lacked two prerequisites: capital and brains. The upper class had an aversion to all participation in business activity. For example, one prominent Hungarian had confided that in his circles he was looked upon as having "strayed" because he was now occupying himself as a wholesaler in textiles.

By 1942, about 299,000 acres of farmland had been expropriated from Jews and sold. Tens of thousands of Jews had no work at all. Once the war started, that slack was taken up by throwing the unemployed Jews into forced labor. Jews were drafted into the army as "auxiliary" labor. They couldn't fight, but they did wear Hungarian-army uniforms. (This infuriated the Germans when both armies found themselves on the Russian front together.)

The Jews of Europe were being destroyed in German killing centers. Still the Jews of Hungary remained. Between March 1939 and late 1944, Hungary had three prime ministers. One was extremely pro-German. The others were reluctantly aligned with the Third Reich.

The third, a reluctant, was Miklos Kallay, who took office in March 1942. He was the first prime minister whom Berlin actually asked to deport Jews as part of the Final Solution. Kallay would not. He stalled. He delayed. He made concessions. No Hungarian Jew was sent to a death camp while he was in power.

If Germany demanded that Jews wear the Star of David, Kallay protested that the Romanian Jews were not made to do likewise. If Berlin wanted the Jews deported, Kallay wanted to know whether Italian Jews were getting the same treatment. If Germany asked that the Jews be made ready for evacuation to Poland, the request was met with a question—was the same happening in Italy?

At one point when Germany asked that all Jews be confined in labor camps or ghettos, Kallay responded, "The incarceration of Jews in labor camps and ghettos cannot be carried out within the existing framework of legal norms."

In March 1944, Hitler summoned regent Admiral Horthy, now in his seventies, to Klessheim Castle. There Horthy was given an ultimatum. Either Horthy would establish a pro-German government or Hitler's army would occupy Hungary.

Horthy made his choice.

Kallay was out. And so were the Jews.

6

It could have been any one of so many evenings, the family sitting around our huge kitchen table, talking over the day after a light meal that was our supper. It was quiet and warm, calm and nice, a time to be lulled into believing everything was good and right.

Even at the age of fourteen, I could tell things were changing, becoming edgy and perplexing. Something was very wrong, but whatever it was, it was outside the safety of my family, my kitchen, my house, the house that had been my grandparents'.

But that evening turned out to be very different from any other evening. Apuka had made his decision.

"I thought we were Hungarian citizens," he said slowly and sadly, as if he didn't believe or trust what he was about to tell us. "I was a soldier. I fought for our country when Hungary needed me. Didn't the poet Vorosmarthy Mihaly write that the heroes who die on the battlefield in defense of the nation have not died in vain? That the nation will remember them and the glory of their achievement will survive in the memory of the nation forever? Who is remembering now? I thought nothing would happen to us. But it has, and we have to leave Tolcsva, because I can't stand it any more. Watching those people on my land, working in my vineyards and fields where I have worked all my life. It isn't right that I can't go there any more! It isn't right, but we do have to leave."

Anyuka didn't argue, not even the smallest objection. I guess she, of all people, knew the torment that my father had been going through. Our fifteen acres had been taken away and distributed in two-acre lots to other people, our neighbors, men that father had dealt with all his life, men he had thought he knew. Not one of them had said, "Hey, listen, this isn't right. This is Zoltan Gluck's land. He's a good man. He's never done anything wrong. Why should you give this to me? It's his."

No, they had taken the land without a single demur, and now Apuka could no longer stand seeing their faces.

We were leaving Tolcsva. Today in the United States, with families moving on the average of every few years, no one thinks much of transplanting a family three thousand miles. In Hungary, then, you didn't move. You were born, endured, and died in the same place. Roots were strong, tangled, and not easily pulled up. Still, I didn't feel anything cataclysmic was taking place. Apuka said move. We were moving. Apuka always knew what to do and when to do it. He always did. Why would he be wrong now?

Besides, there was too much to be done to dwell on fears and misgivings. We had to close up the house in Tolcsva. Decide what we were taking with us. Say goodbye to all my friends at school, though what was "goodbye"? I never doubted that I would be seeing them again soon. Apuka, I was sure, would make everything right, and we would be back home again.

Then there was the new home. A teeny house on Vaji Ut Boulevard in Miskolc, a city, a big city to me, about 140 kilometers from Budapest.

We had two bedrooms, a living room, a kitchen, and an entrance hall. Margaret and I helped clean house—Jews were no longer allowed to have any gentile help. But it was no great hardship, since there wasn't much to do—the house was so tiny.

I didn't make friends, although I did meet people at school. The routine was to come home right after class and stay there. Anyuka didn't trust the city or its streets. She wanted us close, where she could watch us. Besides, wouldn't we be going back to Tolcsva soon? And that would mean leaving the new friends behind.

As it turned out that "next day or the day after" that we were going home turned into two years. Ernoke was Bar Mitzvahed in Miskolc. We got by as it got harder and harder to get by. Apuka had brought our two cows from Tolcsva. We bought six more and made out by selling milk to other Jews. It was forbidden to sell to anyone else.

A lot of things were forbidden, and the list kept getting longer. You found ways around the laws or you did without. For one thing, Jews were not supposed to cut kosher meat any more. But that didn't stop kosher butchering. There are some things that can't be stopped.

We knew someone in a nearby village with kosher meat. It was my job to pedal my bike over and bring back the meat. I was never stopped. My rosey cheeks, my "Gentile" appearance, were probably my protection. And I never thought of what might have happened if I had been caught. A fine? Imprisonment? It was my job to get the meat, so I did.

We no longer had the vineyards or fields. We no longer

had the shoe store. Jews couldn't deal in leather goods any more. (For some reason they were allowed to sell sneakers, probably because the profit margin was so small that the pittance wasn't worth troubling about.) We had to leave our village. Yet we were no worse off than many of our friends and relatives.

Uncle Lajos in Tokay lost his big shoe store, of course. His daughters were reduced to stringing beads as the only way to buy food for the family. They still had their house, since there was no such things as a mortgage. It was theirs outright—or until they fell behind in taxes. They were able to get along on basic living and subsistence. If they didn't have meat, they ate soup. If they didn't have soup, they ate bread. If there was no bread, there was hunger. It was a living, even if there was hardship. If they, those unseen, malevolent forces that passed the insane laws, didn't kill us, everything else could be forgiven, because everything else you could stand. You can't stand against a gun.

We no longer sat around the kitchen table. The kitchen in Miskolc was too small to have one. In a strange sense, the family had lost a little of its magnetic core when it lost that table. The house in Miskolc might have been smaller than the one in Tolcsva, but somehow it made the family more diffuse. That isn't to say it was less loving; it was just somehow different. I guess I missed the kitchen's warmth.

Mother had begun devouring the newspaper, searching for clues to the impossible things that were happening around us.

"Wait, children," she kept saying, sitting in the parlor that doubled as a bedroom for Margaret and me. "This will stop. You'll see—once America moves, this will all end."

As the weeks and months passed and nothing happened,

she began to add, "The only trouble is, America moves very slowly."

Her faith in that distant land of goodness was not due to Aunt Hani's living there. If anything, Anyuka should have felt a touch of bitterness toward Aunt Hani. In 1933, right after America ended its idiotic era of Prohibition, when times happened to be hard for us, Apuka had appealed to Aunt Hani to help us set up an export business to send some of our good wine to the United States. Father had never been a favorite of Hani's, and nothing but silence ever came of it.

So it wasn't Aunt Hani. It was a blind faith in the United States, an almost idolatrous belief that virtue and well-being resided there, if nowhere else.

The United States would save us all.

And then I was fifteen. Tolcsva was starting to lose some of its focus. Life was becoming Miskolc. The tiny house, studying, helping with chores. And being glad that I had Anyuka, Apuka, Margaret, Ernoke, and my sweet little dog Csuli, a gorgeous spitz, whom I loved as much as anything and who was all mine.

I loved my older brother, Icu, too. And I worried about him, although Anyuka told me not to fret. He was safer where he was than he would be at home, she said. Where he was, wasn't exactly clear. He had been conscripted. Not as Apuka had been in World War I. Not to fight side by side with other Hungarians and to come back with the tales of what he had done and how good the men had been to each other. Jews were no longer afforded that luxury. Jews, by judgment of one Adolf Hitler, former house painter, ex-convict, weren't fit to hold a rifle, to be patriotic and love their country, to live decently—or, as it turns out, to live at all. Jews were fit to work, the harder, more arduously, and crueler the better.

Icu had been impressed into the Hungarian army for forced labor. Anyuka reasoned that as long as labor was needed, Icu would be safe and fed. And labor is always needed.

We no sooner got used to a set of bans and rules, than a new set was slapped upon us.

It didn't matter. We lived.

Then it was 1944.

It was the year I was to turn sweet sixteen, when my anyuka had promised the most wonderful sweet-sixteen party for me. Maybe it would be the day I'd first get kissed.

It was 1944.

The world had come to an end, and I didn't even know it.

7

If Admiral Horthy believed that by getting rid of Kallay he was saving Hungarian autonomy, he was greatly mistaken.

Even before the new very pro-Nazi prime minister, Dome Sztojay, had time to form his government and take office on March 22, 1944, Hungary was swarming with German "advisers" —advisers for policy, advisers for the army, advisers in propaganda, advisers in industry. They couldn't be called a shadow government—they were too visible for that.

There were also advisers for the "Jewish problem," orchestrated by Adolf Eichmann. Eichmann was faced with a different type of problem than had been present in other countries. He had a government that up until now had been reluctant and obstructionist when it came to deporting the Jews. And he had a Jewish population that was not totally in the dark about what had been happening in the rest of Europe. As Dr. Rudolf Kastner, a former official of the Hungarian Zionist Organization, was to explain:

> In Budapest we had a unique opportunity to follow the fate of the European Jewry. We had seen how they had been disappearing one after the other from the map of Europe. At the moment of the occupation of Hungary, the number of dead Jews amounted to over five million. . . . We knew

more than was necessary about Auschwitz. . . . We had, as early as 1942, a complete picture of what had been happening in the East with the Jews deported to Auschwitz and the other extermination camps.

The German strategy in other countries had been to keep the victims as much in the dark as possible. Then, when they were told that the trains were going to labor camps, Jews boarded them docilely. Had they known the true destination, conceivably there would have been uprising and escape attempts.

But in Hungary, Eichmann was faced with knowledge, at least knowledge possessed by the Jewish leaders. To overcome this, he had some of his SS men set up a preliminary meeting with the leaders in Budapest. Some of the Jews showed up with suitcases, prepared to go marching off to their deaths.

"Oh, no—no one is going to be arrested," they were assured. No, the purpose of the meeting was only to tell the Jews that they must set up a council, a *Judenrat*, which had to make a list of all Jewish property. That was all.

And that seemed to be all, except each day brought some new request. Jews must relinquish their typewriters. Their toilet water. Blankets. Mirrors.

On March 31, Eichmann himself met with the leaders to outline the function of the Judenrat—which was basically to serve as a conduit for German orders—and to reassure the Jews that no mistreatment would take place.

The Jewish leaders wanted to believe. So they did.

The other half of Eichmann's problem was the Hungarian government, but that resolved itself when Sztojay simply pushed through all German directives. Jews could no longer be journalists, civil servants, notaries, musicians, accountants, lawyers. Only doctors were allowed to keep practicing, since one-third of all the doctors in Hungary were Jewish. Jewish banks were closed, as were Jewish stores and bank accounts.

Jewish property of all types was confiscated, and limits were put on the amount and kind of food Jews could buy. Curfews were instituted. And then, beginning March 29, 1944, all Jews were required to wear the yellow Star of David.

It was time. Eichmann could start his ghettoization plan, the first step on the road to Auschwitz.

8

I was standing in front our little house, watching Csuli watching the world. He sat there beautifully, his long white hair so clean, his feathery tail so perky.

I didn't like going out much. There had been some rock throwing and name calling. Ernoke had even received a terrible cut on his forehead the previous winter from a rock-filled snowball. Even though there was always something to worry about, I found being with Csuli enough of a pleasure to overcome most anxieties.

Csuli's little ears perked up. There was a noise coming from up the street. It got louder and louder.

"Anyuka! Apuka! Quickly! Come quickly! There are tanks and jeeps and soldiers!"

Sometimes it takes only a fraction of a moment for everything to change. One second I was standing on a quiet street with my wonderful little dog. The next second the street was filled terrifying, fearful machines and my little Csuli had run forward to growl and protect me.

It was over immediately.

The first jeep smashed into Csuli, obliterating his whiteness, turning him into a gory mass of dirt and marrow and bone splinters and tattered fur and blood.

The jeeps and tanks kept rolling by as we stood, my family and me, and other families on the block, watching, numbed.

March 19, 1944.

We heard the Germans were coming in, were taking over Hungary. We sat in our house all day, saying next to nothing. We just looked at one another. We didn't know what was coming next. We didn't have the answers, because we didn't have the questions. We were stunned.

Finally Apuka spoke. "Anyuka, you are to take the children back to Tolcsva. Maybe they will be safer there. After all, we have friends there. People know us there. They won't let anything happen. I'll come tomorrow after I see what can be salvaged here. I'll close the house and join you tomorrow."

Going back to Tolcsva! I had dreamed about it for so long.

We packed everything we could into tablecloths, which we then tied at the corners and carried on our backs like knapsacks.

A streetcar to the train station. Buy tickets. Wait. Other people seemed to be living a normal day. There weren't many in that great glass cavern of a station. Those there were conducting themselves as if it were just any day, not a day filled with anguish and shattered like my poor little Csuli. Not a day of uncertainty. Why couldn't Apuka come with us? Would he be able to join us? Would he be able to find out what was going on?

At last it was time to board the train. We took our places on the hard wooden benches in third class, Anyuka, Margaret, Ernoke, and me. Nothing much was said in the two hours the trip took, although Anyuka would occasionally say something, more talking out loud than talking to us.

"We'll get to Tolcsva, and we'll keep quiet. Everything will be fine. Oh, I don't even know why we're going to Tolcsva, but Apuka says we should go, so maybe we'll be all right."

The train clattered on through the darkness. And then it stopped.

I snapped up.

"Anyuka, we've arrived. Let's get off the train."

She looked out the window.

"But Lily, I can't see the station. We can't possibly be there—there's no light."

"No, no. We're at the back of the train. The front is in the station, and the engineer must not have pulled in far enough."

"Lily, how could you know that? Let's ask the conductor. He'll surely know if we've reached Tolcsva or not."

"Anyuka, I've ridden this train so many times with Apuka; don't you think I'd know if we've arrived or not?"

I had her there. I was the adventurer. I was the one who went on all the trips.

We got off the train. It pulled away. And we were in the middle of nowhere, in the dark.

"Now look!" Anyuka was more than a little exasperated, with every right to be. "We aren't in the station. What are we going to do?"

That seemed like a silly question to me.

"We'll walk along the tracks. There's not another train due until tomorrow. We'll walk until we get to Tolcsva."

So we walked, with our heavy tablescloths, picking our way from track tie to track tie. It was hard going. After a while we left the tracks and started walking along a road that paralleled them.

"Children, we'll never make Tolcsva tonight. It's better that we go to Aunt Eszti's in Lizka [Olaszliska]. She's closer and she'll be able to put us up for one night."

We were all relieved and actually were beginning to feel a bit merry. The anxiety of Miskolc was fading. We would get to Aunt Eszti's soon and have something to eat.

"Immediately!" Anyuka growled at us. "Into the ditches." We scrambled and slid and were out of sight before the trucks and jeeps passed us. They were army vehicles.

I don't know why Anyuka thought they would recognize us as Jews, but she did, and she feared we were breaking a curfew and would be shot on the spot.

We barely made Aunt Eszti's by daybreak. Waves of trucks and jeeps kept coming. When they did, we went back into the ditches.

Our stay at Aunt Ezsti's was a fatigued blur. I would wake up to hear her and mother whispering with fright, and then I would be asleep again, dreaming of Csuli running through our vineyards in Tolcsva.

We got home the next day. We were tired, but we had to get the house opened up and clean. Then we had to wait for Apuka.

It took him a few days. He had to bring the cows. How else would we live if we didn't have our cows?

We had returned to our kitchen table. Apuka didn't have much to tell. His days had been relatively uneventful.

"And your trip? Did you have any trouble?" he asked us.

"Well, we're safe and we're here," Anyuka answered. "But it did take us a little longer than expected. We got off the train before it arrived in the station."

"You what? You mean it was a few meters from the station, or something like that?"

"Not exactly. You see, Lily here was sure we had arrived, so we got off. And then we walked on the tracks to where they meet the road."

"Oh, no, Anyuka, do you know where you were?" Apuka was white and almost trembling. "You got off on the railroad bridge. One wrong step and you would have been killed in the fall or drowned in the river."

I shivered, wondering why I had wanted so badly to get off the train.

We celebrated Passover, the happiest of festivals, in Tolcsva. At the seders, the ceremonial evening meals, we ate matzoh, the unleavened bread that symbolizes the Jewish flight from Egypt. We had charoses, the reddish mixture of grated apples and walnuts mixed with sweet wine, which serves as a reminder of the bricks Jews made while slaves in Egypt. We rejoiced that although the pharaoh ordered the first-born Jewish boys killed, the race had survived, as Jews always would survive.

9

Hungary was divided into five zones plus Budapest. It was Eichmann's plan that starting with the Carpathian zone, because it was the closest to the advancing Soviet troops, all Jews from villages with fewer than ten thousand inhabitants would be centralized in certain designated ghetto towns.

Once ghettoization was completed in one zone, the Jews would be shipped out to Auschwitz as ghettoization began in the next.

His original timetable was:

		Begin Ghettoization	*Deportation Ends*
Zone 1	Carpathians	April 16	June 7
Zone 2	Transylvania	May 4	June 7
Zone 3	North of Budapest from Kosice to Reich frontier	June 7	June 17
Zone 4	East of Danube without Budapest	June 17	June 30
Zone 5	West of Danube without Budapest	June 29	July 9
Budapest		early July	end of July

Rounding up the Jews and herding them into the ghettos would be carried out by Hungarian police. The Germans were to have as little to do with it as possible.

Only in Budapest would there not be a specific ghetto area. The Hungarian government felt that would be an open invitation for the Allies to bomb the rest of the city. But certain houses were designated as Jewish buildings. The Jews were forced out of their own homes and into these.

Here is a list of all the villages that sent their Jews to the ghetto in Sátoraljaújhely. Each area had similar lists, with other larger towns acting as the magnet.

Sátoraljaújhely

Agard	Kiràlyhelmec	Semjen
Bekecs	Kiskovesd	Szegilong
Berecki	Kisrozvagy	Szephalom
Bodroghalom	Laca	Szerdahely
Bodrogkeresztur	Legyesbenye	Szerencs
Bodzasujlak	Mad	Szomotor
Cigand	Magyarsas	Taktaharkany
Cseke	Megysszo	Talya
Damoc	Mikohaza	Tarcal
Dombrad	Monok	Tiszakarad
Erdobenye	Nagykovesd	Tiszaluc
Garany	Nagyrozvacy	Tokay
Gesztely	Olaszliska	Tolcsva
Golop	Onod	Ujcsanalos
Hernadnemeti	Pacin	Vamosujfalu
Karos	Revleanyvar	Vajdacska
Kaso	Ricse	Zalkod
	Saruspatak	Zombor

10

Mayor Szalai's man, Szotak, the town crier, was in the street shouting something, something about Jews.

It was the day after Passover. I was still feeling full and contented. Maybe it wasn't as it used to be, and some of our furniture was still in Miskolc, but still there was enough there to make me feel we had at last come home.

What could that fool crier be shouting about? We went to the windows.

"All Jews to the schoolhouse in two hours. All Jews are leaving Tolcsva in two hours."

It was absurd. The man must have been drunk, I thought. But then I saw the look that hung between my Anyuka and Apuka. They didn't think he was drunk. They were taking what he shouted very seriously.

"Wait here," Apuka ordered. "I will find out what this is about."

Before he could, there was a knock at the door. Two policemen were outside.

"You are Jews living here." It wasn't a question. Everyone in Tolcsva knew we were Jewish. Everyone in Tolcsva knew everything about everyone else.

"Be standing outside your house in two hours. Have with you only some clothes and food. Don't try to take anything else. You'll then be told where to go and what to do. It will go very badly for you if you trying running or hiding. Remember, two hours."

They were gone.

How could we be leaving? We had only just got back. And what clothes should we take?

"No, Lily, not your tennis racquet dress. It's too small for you now. Take something practical," Anyuka told me in an everyday, unemotional voice.

Everything was so calm. Anyuka and Apuka were quietly getting bundles together. All that delicious food left over from Passover. A few pieces of clothing. Quietly, methodically. Apuka got our little brass urn, filled with the few pieces of jewelry and other items of value we had. He went to the back with his shovel, dug a hole, buried it.

Why doesn't he dig up his gun from World War 1? I wondered. *Then he could shoot those people if they come back.*

Apuka didn't dig up anything. He went back into the house.

We waited, saying nothing. Waited.

We didn't even put our dishes from breakfast away. They stayed where they were.

Two hours are a lifetime when you're mentally ticking off each second.

Finally, time was up.

We picked up our bundles and went outside. Nothing was making any sense. Not our standing there. Not our neighbors standing in front of their houses. Especially not our neighbors, our non-Jewish neighbors, who suddenly appeared out of nowhere and swarmed, laughing, into our house, grabbing at our belongings—our clothes, pots, pans, even the breakfast dishes. Whatever wasn't nailed down was theirs.

I clutched the little prayer book I had taken, despite the order to take only clothing and food, fearing that someone might grab it from my hand. But there were more valuable and precious things to be had. Then the locust swarm swirled out and down the block to the next house.

The guards arrived, and we were marched to the school-yard, where a muster of horse-drawn wagons, fifteen, twenty, had been assembled. We knew those wagons, and we knew those wagoneers. Hadn't some of them taken our grapes from the fields to the cellars? Hadn't thay taken our grain to the mill?

Where were they taking us now?

The three hundred and fifty Jews of Tolcsva had no idea. They waited until the ten or twelve guards, all Hungarian police, pushed and herded us into the wagons, fifteen people squashed into each.

The procession began moving through the streets, slowly, as if to give the rest of Tolcsva adequate time to laugh, hoot, and yell vile taunts. And there among them, laughing as loud and as crassly as any of them, was the midwife who had delivered so many of the children now being carted away.

There were some who stood silently. And I did see a couple of people crying. But for the most part it was Christmas and New Years and the end of harvest wrapped into one for Tolcsva.

What had we ever done to them?

11

You can adjust to almost anything, if you have to.

Thousands of people from fifty-two villages shoe-horned into one section of Sátoraljaújhely. Five families crammed into one room. Wall-to-wall mattresses. All the families in all the rooms sharing one kitchen.

You got by. You made do. You kept everything as clean as possible to prevent the start of some disease from over-crowding. You survived.

There was always someone, some leader to organize and keep things running. The doctors who had been thrown into the ghetto set up a system of visiting everyone, to check them for disease and lice. I volunteered to help, trudging through those six square blocks that had become prison for some twelve thousand people. There were no brick and mortar walls around their jail, no barbed wire or fences, only armed guards, fellow countrymen, who patrolled the streets and didn't let you go beyond a certain point.

I used to sneak out to buy food. Our Passover leftovers had not lasted long. I would hold my pocketbook against my left side to hide the yellow Star of David that Anyuka had sewn on my dress when we were still in Tolcsva.

I didn't always fool our jailers. Their mocking laughter would sound out. "Take your bag away from your side, Jew!" they'd call. "Why are you covering up your star? We know you're a Jew even if you don't look like one." The green rooster feathers in their hats shook with each word and laugh.

I was not afraid of them. I walked by calmly, unemotionally, erect, as if they weren't there. I knew I must go on. The family needed food. Only once was Apuka allowed to go to Tolcsva to get something for us to eat. After that we subsisted on my little forays. Once I went to Tolcsva also. I had the papers of our former maid, identifying her as Aryan. She had left them in the house in Tolcsva, and Apuka had had the foresight to throw them in with the few things we brought. I figured if I was stopped, I would produce them. But I wasn't stopped, and I came back with food and flowers.

My school friend Editt wearing the Star of David.

לזכר עולם

לקדושי קהילת

ש. א. אוּיהל הי״ד

‹ והסביבה› מחוז זמפלין הונגריה›

SÁTORALJA UJHELY

ÉS ZEMPLÉN MEGYE HITKÖZSÉGEI

שנספו בשנת השואה תש״ד

ע״י הנאצים וגרוריהם ימ״ש

ימי הזכרון ט״ו-כ׳ בסיון

ת נ צ ב ה

מנציחים ארגון יוצאי ש. א. אוּיהל

והסביבה בישראל ובתפוצות

A memorial plaque to the Jews of the Sátoraljaújhely ghetto. It reads:

"In everlasting memory of the sanctified community of Sátoraljaújhely and the surrounding County Zemplén, Hungary, which died in the year of the Holocaust 1944/5704 at the hands of the Nazis and their accomplices (may their memory be erased).

"Days of remembrance, the 15th through the 20th in the month of Sivan.

"May their souls be bound up in the bond of life."

Every time I returned from these trips, Icu, who had had been sent back from the army labor camp, would say, "Lily, next time don't come back. Run away, hide—anything, but stay away."

Every time I answered, "No. Whatever happens to my family must happen to me."

In the middle of May the first trains left for Auschwitz. Families disappeared every day. They were there, and then they weren't.

Each day grew darker.

The father of Rozsi Grunfeld, a Tolcsva school friend, slashed his wrists and then begged his daughter to let him bleed to death. But how could Rozsi let the life of any man, and most especially her father, ooze away with each drop of blood, even though she suspected that the nearest future held no hope, that what would happen to him might be worse than what was already happening to him?

Rozsi got help. Her father was given a transfusion and patched up in the ghetto's makeshift hospital so that he could take his place on the next transport to Auschwitz.

Our house became less and less crowded as more families disappeared. The ghetto began to take on a ghost-town appearance in comparison to the teems of humanity that had been there before.

Then our name was called. The Glucks were to be on the next transport, the last transport from Sátoraljaújhely.

12

We were without protection, standing on the threshold of our destruction.

I am asking you, were we Jews people to be jealous of? Were we Jews people hated for their brilliance? For their tenacity?

We stood without resistance, subjects of ridicule and hatred. We were struck, stunned, overcome by the tremendous tragedy befalling us, helpless from infant to most elderly, from sick to healthy, weak to strong, all helpless.

We stood waiting to go to our destruction, to deaths with no memorial candles because there would be no graves. The only memorial lights for these victims would be those burning in the hearts of survivors. Those lights were not to be extinguished.

Anyuka added thick sweet wine to the cookies she baked, to give them more nourishment.

"If we are going to work," she said, "these cookies will give us strength and keep us from hunger."

There wasn't much time to prepare for our trip, but Anyuka did what she could. She sewed extra cloth under

75

our shirts, in case where we were going was cold. She put little name tags on our collars, in case we got separated or lost. Apuka made a special blanket for Ernoke, lined with pieces of sheepskin and wool. He rolled it up and attached carrying straps on the outside so it would be easier to carry. We didn't know what else we would be made to carry or what we would be made to do.

The morning we were to leave, two policemen came to the house. There were so few people left in the ghetto, gathering them up would be a short, easy job.

They searched us, humiliating body searches as if we were the most common criminals. When the policemen reached Ernoke, one took an interest in the new blanket. Roughly, he tried pulling it from Ernoke's back. When it didn't come off quickly enough, the man gave the boy a dreadful kick.

Apuka went for the blanket, which was now on the ground, hoping that the policeman had used it as an excuse for the kick and wasn't actually interested in it. Whether Apuka was right or wrong didn't matter. The second policeman saw the move, unfurled his leather bullwhip—and one, two, three shirt- and flesh-ripping lashes went across Apuka's back. Apuka began a terrible moan. We did nothing. The right to comfort had been taken from us.

Was this actually happening to us?

After everyone was searched, we were marched to the railroad tracks, where cattle cars waited for their consignments. Fifty people to a car. Small windows cross-hatched with chicken wire. One barrel in the middle for a toilet. Room to sit down, shoulder to shoulder, hip to hip.

Packed in. The doors shut.

Our journey had begun.

13

Two hundred and ninety thousand Jews were collected and shipped out of zones 1 and 2 by June 7, 1944.

14

It was the smell. The thick, dark, acrid smell of souring human wastes.

For two and a half days we were in that cattle car, never permitted to get out. In fact, we saw daylight only once, when the train stopped in Kassa, a town on our northbound route. The doors were opened. We were handed a little fresh water. The doors were locked again.

I tried not to use the barrel. The closer you got to it, the more overpowering it was. I don't think I was the only one trying to curb natural functions. But in two and a half days, sooner or later, you had to get near the reeking thing, you had to use it.

We did not know how long the train ride would be. We did not know where it was going. Anyuka was careful to dole out the little food we had frugally. We didn't know how long we would have to make it last.

Uncle Lajos and Aunt Boriska from Tokay were on the same train with us, in the same car. It was something of a comfort to have them there with Cousins Irene, Kato, and Rozsi, too. What was going to happen would happen to all of us. Maybe we would be able to help each other in what was to come, get us through whatever was waiting at the end of the ride.

There wasn't much talking. There wasn't much to talk about. There was praying and some crying.

Early in the morning of the third day, the train stopped. With a jolt and a thud the cars came to a halt.

Clank. The doors opened and we saw there was still a world outside, a dark, hazy, gloomy morning.

Up until now it had been Hungarian soldiers and police who had given us orders. Now our guards were Germans, yelling, "*Schnell!* Quick! In a hurry! *Steh' auf, verfluchtene Juden!* Stand in line, Jews! Five in a row. Men here. Women here. Boys there. Girls over there."

There was no time for panic. Orders were being yelled too quickly and too loudly. Mothers clutched children. Fathers stood helpless. We were bewildered. There were so many people getting off the train.

"Don't worry about your families. You'll see them later. Now separate."

I looked for a station sign and couldn't find one. The world was ending in a station without a name.

The guards were shouting a litany of promises. "You'll meet your families later. . . . You will get meat twice a week. . . . New clothing . . . better than home. . . . Just get in line. . . . Just do your work. . . . Do what you are told."

Apuka and my brothers were shunted off, Ernoke to one group, the older two to another. Seeing the division, Anyuka hurriedly tied a kerchief to my head.

"This will make you look older," she whispered frantically. "Stay with the women. Stay with me."

I *couldn't* stay with her. The lines of five across advanced toward a table where several people sat. It was the one in the middle who made the decision, who decided the fates. When our line reached the front, with a cock of the head, he sent Anyuka, Aunt Boriska, and Rozsi to the right, across the tracks away from us.

With a slight movement of his head, the infamous Doctor Mengele had robbed me of my mother. Margaret, Kato, Irene, and I were motioned left, but not before I saw Aunt Boriska faint, falling onto the tracks. Anyuka tried to lift her. Immediately an SS guard was prodding her with a rifle butt, making her move on. Then she was beyond the train, out of sight. Aunt Boriska was dragged away.

My father and brothers had disappeared. I didn't have a chance to wave or smile or say a prayer for any of them.

We were marched into camp, across a huge square decorated with poles topped with human skulls and signs that said *"Arbeit macht frei"* (Work makes you free).

There were hundreds of us, dazedly obeying what the SS guards, male and female, told us to do. They brandished their bullwhips and yelled commands. What else could we do but obey? There was not time for recalcitrance or resistance—we could only follow the orders and march into a huge hall.

In it hundreds and hundreds of women were undressing, sorting, and throwing clothes into piles. Shoes. Shirts. Coats. Dresses. It looked as if the whole world had been undressed. It seemed like millions and millions of pieces of clothes, as if it were some kind of surrealistic rummage sale. Shoes as if the world had taken off its shoes. Shirts as if there were none left anywhere else. Shirt mountains. Panty mountains. Handkerchief and prayer-book hills.

And still more women streamed into the hall, undressed, and added their things to the mountains.

The cacophony was stomach turning. Enveloping and abusing, it overwhelmed and broke you down. The *Kapos*, prisoner-helpers, went down the lines of naked women, taking anything else deemed valuable—rings, false teeth with gold in them. They took earrings from Margaret and me that we had worn since birth.

Then it was form a single line, advance slowly, to the *Kapos* with clippers. Within seconds, my long, beautiful braids, which had hung to my waist, were gone. All my hair was gone. I looked at my sister. I wasn't sure it was Margaret any more. I wasn't sure it was me. We all looked like inmates in a mental institution who had years ago lost all touch with reality.

We were marched into another room. Margaret, Irene, Kato, and I tried to keep close for safety in this hell.

If the noise in the hall had been next to unbearable, the torture in this room was the heat, coming from some unseen source.

"Sit on the floor. Be quiet."

Bald, overheated, naked, disoriented, horrified, scared, we were quiet and we waited.

Don't think about the heat, I said to myself, *and it won't be so bad. Don't think about anything.*

The heat didn't lessen. I saw that Margaret was about to swoon. If she did, what would the guards do, take her away? Already I could see that weakness must not be shown. I had to take care of Margaret. I had to keep her from fainting.

Across the room, way over in the corner, was a faucet. Without hesitation, I scrambled over naked legs and laps to get to it. It worked, and the water was cold. In my cupped hands, I cradled a few drops and made my way back to

Margaret. I splashed the water on her face, and she revived. I was lucky and fast. No guard had seen me.

Time passed. Hours? Yes. How many? I don't know. Something shy of eternity, but not by much.

"Up and in line."

We were taken into a communal shower room, open, with no stalls, drains in the floor, naked showerheads coming out of the wall. We didn't know that sometimes it wasn't water that came out of those heads. Sometimes it was gas. We didn't know and at that point, I'm not sure we would have cared. It was enough to be doing something besides sitting and waiting.

The water was icy cold, as cold as the Patak in winter, so cold it burned. It didn't matter—we weren't in it very long, only long enough to remind us what clean had once been.

After the shower, gray dresses, gray-striped undershirts, and wooden shoes were handed out. We were allowed to dress.

We were led outside to the square. Lined up in our rows of five. There we had our first taste of *Zell Appell*.

15

Before the outbreak of the war, Germany had created concentration camps for three types of prisoners: political
(including those overheard making anti-fascist remarks); habitual
criminals and sex offenders; and certain Jews.

Once the war began, however, Hitler shifted his Final
Solution, the elimination of all Jews from Europe, into overdrive.
Concentration camps became killing centers.

As Heinrich Himmler told Rudolf Hess, the camp commandant of Auschwitz, "The Führer has given the order for a
final solution of the Jewish Question. . . . We, the SS, must
carry out that order."

When considering the Final Solution, it should be remembered
that throughout history people have been killed and murdered
—because they were combatants in war; because they held
something other people wanted; because they were invaders or
conquerors; because they were in the way of others trying to
reclaim something. But the Final Solution was a case of an entire
people being killed, not for anything they had done, not because
of anything they were proseltyzing, not for anything they were
trying to revolutionize. They were killed because they were
there and not for any other reason.

There were six major killing centers, which had 165

auxiliary labor camps—Kulmhof, in Wartheland; Belzec and Sobibor, in the Lublin area; Lublin itself; Treblinka, near Warsaw; and Auschwitz, in upper Silesia.

On entering the camps, some Jews were allowed to live— about 10 percent, to maintain the camps, for labor in industry, or because too many people arrived on a given day to be handled in the gas chambers and crematoriums. However, the primary purpose of these centers was death.

To exterminate as many as possible as quickly as possible took a great deal of complex organization. As Raul Hilberg explained:

> The killing centers worked quickly and efficiently: a man would step off a train in the morning, and in the evening his corpse was burned and his clothes packed away for shipment to Germany. Such an operation was the product of a great deal of planning, for the death camp was an intricate mechanism in which a whole army of specialists played their parts. Viewed superficially, this smoothly functioning apparatus is deceptively simple, but upon closer examination the operations of the killing center resemble in several respects the complex mass-production methods of a modern plant. . . .
>
> The most striking fact about the killing center operation is that, unlike the earlier phases of the destruction process [shootings and starvation], they were unprecedented. Never before in history had people been killed on an "assembly line" basis. The killing center . . . has no prototype, no administrative ancestor. This is explained by the fact that it was a composite institution which consisted of two parts, the camp proper and the killing installations in the camp. . . . As separate establishments, both the concentration camp and the gas chamber had been in existence for some time. The great innovation was effected when the two devices were fused.

In Auschwitz they were so well fused that two of the furnaces were built with gas chambers underneath them. The chambers, called *Leichkeller*, or corpse cellars, could hold up to two thousand people. Immediately after the victims were gassed, their corpses were taken by elevator up into the furnaces above.

Another item that increased the efficiency of Auschwitz, making it possible for at least two and a half million people to have been killed there, was the use of a new gas. Carbon monoxide, used elsewhere, proved to be slow and messy. It could take up to two or three hours to kill everyone in the chamber. As one survivor described it, the bodies "were thrown out blue, wet with sweat and urine, the legs covered with excrement and menstrual blood," making disposal more difficult.

In Auschwitz a gas called Zyklon B, a prussic acid, was used instead of carbon monoxide. When poured through the shafts of the chamber, Zyklon B changed quickly from solid to a gas. Zyklon B had been used for years as a rat and bug killer. It proved very efficient on humans, so efficient that once it was poured down the shaft, a camp chief with a stop-watch would time how long it took to work.

Again, Raul Hilberg's description:

As the first pellets sublimated on the floor of the chamber, the law of the jungle took over. To escape from the rapidly rising gas, the stronger knocked down the weaker, stepping on the prostrate victims in order to prolong their life by reaching the gas-free layers of air. The agony lasted about two minutes, then the shrieking subsided, the dying men slumped over. Within four minutes everybody in the gas chamber was dead. The gas was never allowed to escape, and after about a half hour the doors were opened. The bodies were found in tower-like heaps, some in sitting or half sitting position under the doors. The corpses were pink in color, with green spots. Some had foam on their lips; others bled through the nose.

About the only problem the Germans had with Zyklon B was one of supply. It could not be stockpiled since it deteriorated within a few months. This meant new supplies had to arrive at Auschwitz on a regular basis. Transportation of the poison proved more difficult as the Third Reich's war efforts deteriorated. Indeed, Eichmann's schedule for the extermination of the Hungarian Jews was thrown off slightly when a shipment foul-up occurred in March 1944. It was quickly straightened out and the deportations began.

The few arriving in Auschwitz who were allowed to live were packed into blocks of primitive barracks. They were the healthiest and strongest, although after living as they did with starvation rations and overcrowding, many did not remain healthy for long. One block, Block 25, had been designed for five hundred prisoners. At one point two thousand were squeezed into it.

16

Zell Appell was a torture, standing at rigid attention for hours and hours and hours and hours until time had no reference point, not being allowed to move or relax, with your muscles getting tighter and tauter, protesting the painful inactivity, not being allowed to do anything except stand, at rigid attention. If you moved, you were beaten back into place and position.

Kapos counted their herd. They prodded them back into straight lines. They kept them standing.

We stood for the entire first night. It had been our first twenty-four hours in Auschwitz, and we still didn't know where we were. Toward daybreak some of the Polish *Kapo* girls took pity on us and whispered down the lines, "Poland. You're in Poland, and this is Auschwitz."

The *Kapos* worked for the Germans, under German orders and observation. They were also our conduits of information, our guides, teachers, and enlighteners, although at first what they told us was beyond comprehension, beyond anything we wanted to believe.

They pointed toward smoke, toward where Anyuka had gone. "Those are the gas chambers. Those chimneys, they are for the crematoriums. That's where your families went. It's where we all might go at any time."

Some of the *Kapos* had been in the camp for years. We knew that, and we knew that they must have seen everything and must know everything. Yet accepting that Anyuka, Apuka, little Ernoke, and Icu had met such a fate? No, that could not be entertained as possible. The German guards said our families had been sent to work. At the beginniing that was what we believed. We had to.

We still didn't know what was to happen to us. We weren't given the tattoo that everyone else got. We were told each night that we would be tattooed the next day, as if it were something to look forward to. Was this Auschwitz a way stop or a destination? The *Kapos* had told us, "You may be sent somewhere else to work, or you might stay here in Auschwitz, or they might change their mind and gas you yet."

We were put in Lager C, one of the camp divisions with its many blocks, or barracks. We were Lager C, Block 10. Each day was the same. Stand in *Zell Appell*, watch the smoke coming from the crematoriums, hear the anguished cries from the gas chambers, hope that some guard wouldn't order you out of line, and wait. That's what we did the most: wait. It seemed, as the days passed, that it hadn't been decided what was to be done with us. New arrivals came and disappeared, and still we stood in *Zell Appell*.

Once a day we were marched to the latrines, such as they were—long ditches with poles running over them lengthwise. We had to straddle the pole, under the eyes of the SS guards. This was our "outing." On the way back to the block we would sometimes pass the *Scheisskommando*, a privileged group who cleaned out the ditch and hauled away the excrement. We weren't supposed to talk to them. Sometimes I couldn't help myself. I would dare to ask some emaciated shell of a man if he had seen my father or brother, if he knew anyone from Tolcsva. I never got an answer. That never stopped me from asking when I got a chance.

At night, in the block, we got our one bowl of wretched beet soup, laced with some medication to stop menstruation. You couldn't swallow the soup; you had to gag it down.

One night the *Kapos* handed out airgram-like paper and pencils.

"You are to write your families in the work camp. They are anxious to hear from you, so tell them that all is well."

Margaret was overjoyed. She took the chance of whispering to me, "See, I told you. Those Polish girls were wrong. Our families didn't go into any gas chamber. Why else would we be writing?"

I should have felt joyous too. What Margaret said was rational and logical. Why would this paper be wasted on dead people? I wanted to believe that, and yet nothing else was rational and logical. I knew that the Polish girls had not lied; still, I was worried about Margaret. She had been giving up. She needed hope.

"You're right, Margaret. Obviously the *Kapos* didn't know what were they talking about."

I left it at that.

The tedious fear had been wearing away my sister. I couldn't comfort her much, for we couldn't talk much. If the Germans had realized that the four of us were related, they would have pulled us apart. Some of us would have followed

Anyuka's route. You were never safe. Each day more selections were made, people weeded out, mothers torn from daughters and discarded. You couldn't show too much attention to someone else. That made the Germans suspicious you were related. They wanted no families together. They wanted you alone and helpless, a solitary spectator to their tableau of terror and indignity.

We were lucky. We managed to fool the guards even though each morning, when we had to line up for *Zell Appell*, always five across, the four of us were always on the same line, always together.

Being together was some comfort, our only comfort.

One day we asked some new arrivals where they were from. They had come from Miskolc, Uncle Bernath's and Aunt Ilonka's home.

"Do you know Manyi Roth?" I asked. "She's my cousin."

"Yes, she's here. I think she's in that block across the way."

Of course, it was forbidden to visit other blocks. And of course, I went anyway.

On the way to the latrine, I dropped out of line and went to the block the girls had indicated.

Manyi was there and looking very sick.

"Oh, Cousin, where is your mother, Ilonka? Isn't she with you? Some of the girls have their mothers in our block."

"I am alone. It is just me."

We talked for a few seconds. I wanted to find out whatever I could about the others. There wasn't much time. Even the few seconds carried a death penalty if I was caught. I had to get back to my own block.

Before I left, Manyi gave me two slices of bread—with

butter. I've always wondered where she got them. I never found out, for that was the last time I ever saw her.

It was June 20, 1944, my sixteenth birthday. As I stood *Zell Appell,* I thought back to that day four years earlier. Anyuka had made cheesecake, *madarteja* (a custardy sweet), fruit preserves, and a seven-layer cake. It had taken her hours to make all these scrumptious treats for my first party.

My eleven friends and I left not a crumb. It was wonderful. Then we played our favorite game, *kint a barany bent a farkas.* It was a circle game with the "wolf" on the inside trying to catch the "sheep" surrounding him. The sun was shining as we raced around, its rays warm and blessing us.

At the end of the party I thanked Anyuka. "This has been the loveliest, most memorable day of my life."

"You're a big girl today," she answered. "You are twelve years old. But I promise you I will make you a bigger party for your sweet sixteen. Just wait and see."

I could hear her saying those words as if she were standing next to me in *Zell Appell.* I could feel her pulse, hear her breath. Sometimes it was the pulse and breath of my mother at my party. Sometimes it was the pulse of someone walking in the shadow of death, the breath of someone gasping gas, not air. What kind of birthday party was I having that day? This time the sheep were in the middle, surrounded by wolves with whips and guns and brutality. If only I could supplant their faces with the face of my Anyuka on the earlier day, pleased, fulfilled, smiling a smile of reassurance and security that only a mother could radiate.

Margaret nudged me. "Lily, be careful. Something is happening down the line."

At first it looked like just one more inspection. This time it was different. There was someone obviously important coming down the lines. He had two girls at his side, an enormous dog, and a whip in his hand.

It was Adolf Eichmann, my birthday present.

17

As Germany's losses increased toward the end of the war, its need for workers to operate the war plants increased also, since every able- and not-so-able-bodied man was being sent to fight at the fronts. It was decided that Jewish prisoners would have to be used to fill in the gaps. Because most of the young Hungarian men had already been drafted into the Hungarian army, the Germans were forced to use Jewish women.

The plan was not a great success. Many industries turned down the offer, saying the women weren't fit for heavy labor. Other industrialists wanted no part of the scheme because they saw that the end of the Third Reich was near, and when the end came, they would have the problem of disposing of the prisoners.

Despite the lack of enthusiasm and acceptance, some Jewish women, a meager few thousand, were pulled out of Auschwitz and sent to work elsewhere.

18

Finally the *Zell Appell* we dreaded arrived.

As long as we were there and standing, we were alive and relatively safe. We knew what each day was.

At this *Zell Appell* we were selected out. Five hundred girls. The four of us. Our end had come, and I accepted it. Surely we would now follow the route of Anyuka and march to those smokestacks.

We were never allowed time for panic and fear. The five hundred were gathered up and moved out. The direction was the railroad tracks, but instead of crossing over them as Anyuka had, we boarded a waiting train of flatbed cars. We scrambled up and sat on boxes loaded on the cars.

What was this all about? Where were we headed? No one knew.

The train was moving before anyone thought to look more closely at the boxes we were perched on. Then a girl who read German read the legend stenciled on each box. "Oh god!" she screamed. "Do you know what is in these boxes? Do you know what that word means?"

She pointed at what was stenciled on each case.

"*Explosives!* We're sitting on explosives!"

Riga, Latvia, near the mouth of the Western Dvina and the Gulf of Riga, an inlet of the Baltic Sea.

It took us two and a half days to get there, always afraid that an Allied plane would swoop down firing, not knowing that we were not the enemy, that we were prisoners.

It was eighty-five degrees afternoons and frigid nights. It was late at night when we arrived and were marched four or five miles through the streets of the big city. I couldn't make out much except that it looked gray and old. There were very few people on the street. Real people wouldn't be out that late. They would be under warm covers in bed. Riga didn't look like a city that knew it was at war.

We were taken to an enormous warehouse-looking structure, fenced and gated to keep out the curious. There must have been three thousand people in that warehouse, political prisoners and Jews, from Lithuania, Poland, Hungary. There simply was no room in the main building for us, so our group, our transport of five hundred, was taken to a stable just beyond. We were put in the loft, with old hay as bedding. Then, as usual, we waited and worried.

There would be no *Zell Appell* here, no selections, beyond weeding out those who grew too fatigued to work. At daybreak we got our first taste of what that work was to be.

A few miles away, at the edge of the city, the Germans were digging in, getting entrenched and ready for the imminent Allied onslaught. More accurately, we were digging in for the Germans. All day we burrowed holes for the soldiers. We hauled the dirt away and cut squares of grass for camouflage, some of which had to be loaded on trucks, to be taken to other entrenchments. The work was arduous and made more so by the tremendous heat in Riga. We didn't dare weaken or tire. The guards were always there, waiting to beat and club at the slightest hint of slacking.

Irene and I were much stronger than our sisters. We could see them getting weaker with each day. Whenever we could, Irene and I would take the places of Margaret and Kato hauling the camouflage to the trucks. It was the worst part of the work. We made the switch as soon as a guard looked away. They never really looked at our faces. They only counted bodies.

It meant more of the harder work for us, but we were not going to take a chance that one of our sisters would get a bullet in the back.

There had been a change in Margaret. She had somehow manufactured an inner strength since the first days in Auschwitz. I was the stronger physically. She had become the stronger emotionally. It wasn't that I was afraid. If something needed to be done, I did it, regardless. I had lost fear. Pessimism had smothered and replaced it. I expected and accepted that each day or move would be death. Margaret was afraid of this pessimism and what it would do to me. To counteract it, she strengthened herself through hope, through a belief that somehow it would end well for us, that we would survive. I was wondering if ending well wasn't death, after all. I could never even approach her belief that somehow what we were enduring was not reality and that we would one day awaken to a bright, clean morning. What was ahead of us would be worse, not better; it would be as terrifying and as horrible as our worst fears.

Margaret would not let me talk this way. She held hope for both of us. I carried the grass for her.

"Lily, you must eat your soup. You have to keep your strength."

Margaret was lecturing me again.

I couldn't eat it. Our rations were *corpa*, wheat-shell gruel that smelled of medicine and repulsive, unidentifiable things. The Germans could make me work, I thought, but they couldn't make me eat.

Besides the one bowl of that abomination, we were given a biscuit or two and black coffee. I would subsist on that, I decided.

What was I to do with the gruel? I wasn't sure where or how to get rid of it. I didn't want to worry Margaret by letting her know I was refusing it. I couldn't give it back or throw it into the street. You never wanted to test the reactions of the Germans. They might think refusing to eat was sabotage. It was clear the only way to dispose of the soup was to toss it down the latrine.

I went to the edge of the latrine closest to the fence that separated the women from the men. There, it was easier to hide what I was doing. It was a wooden fence full of knotholes. You didn't want to look through because chances were there would be a man on the other side, and you didn't want to see what he was doing. Yet, there was always the possibility there would be a man from Tolcsva, someone who had seen Apuka and the boys. It wasn't as if I wanted some kind of naughty peek. That possibility outweighed modesty. I couldn't help looking through.

There was a man there, staring back at me. He wasn't old or young. He was very thin, with skeletal eyes that had seen things I never wanted to see.

"Hello." I was embarrassed getting caught and I was embarrassed by my relative robustness. "Are you Hungarian?"

He wasn't and he didn't speak Hungarian, either. I couldn't make him understand any of my questions at all. I was leaving —I could get caught and punished for talking to someone who was no help at all!—when I realized the man was staring at my bowl, which I hadn't emptied yet, with intense longing.

"Do you want this?"

He didn't understand. I handed the bowl over the fence to him. Quickly he emptied it and handed it back.

I started to go but was held for a second longer by his expression of gratitude, relief, sorrow, and pleasure.

For several nights after, I went back to that spot at the fence with my bowl of slop. He was always there. Then he wasn't. It was just as well. Somehow the soup was smelling better. I began to eat it.

We had no showers or baths, not that they alone would have done much good against the lice infesting the hay. Soon the nipping vermin were all over everyone, in our hair, our clothes. We tried killing them at night, their bites were maddening and potentially deadly if the insects were carrying some disease. There were too many. Finally the guards took us to the sea, where we had to strip, in front of them and anyone else who happened to be watching. The bathing got rid of the lice until we lay down on the hay again. Then they were back, one more torment, one more worry.

It got cooler. It must have been the end of August. One day was like the rest. Excruciating work and tedium. Something to eat. Discussing how we were to keep clean, how we might get rid of the lice. Sleep.

One day, without any kind of warning, the five hundred girls were marched out again, not to the trenches, to some other destination to do only God and the Germans knew what.

19

Widau, on the sea, not far from Riga.

We bathed again and got rid of the lice. Our billet in Widau was a huge warehouse filled with ammunition and food. We weren't there long. Air attacks were increasing and getting nearer. Of course, we had no idea how the war was going. There were no newspapers, no BBC broadcasts, and no time for them even if they had been available. What we did know was that those planes were Allied and inflicting punishment on our persecutors.

"Load up all the food you can carry. We're moving out," came the unexpected order.

Load up all the food you can carry! It was a benediction from heaven. Here we were young women being forced to do inhumanly strenuous labor, while subsisting on next to no food, being told to take all we could carry.

Suddenly our strength and ability to carry multiplied ten-fold. It was chaos as we grabbed bread, large cans of marmalade, and other food intended for German soldiers. We scrambled to get as much as possible. Nothing was too much or too heavy. Off came our undershirts. They were needed to carry more and more food.

After the scramble it was into the lines of five and off. We hadn't got far, when there was an enormous, earth-moving explosion. The warehouse with its ammunition had been blown up to keep it out of Allied hands.

We didn't look back—we were told not to. I knew that the other girls were offering the same silent prayer I was, thanking God that the Germans had decided we were not expendable like the ammunition and blown us up too.

We marched, burdened with the food. Tired, hungry, we didn't stop to enjoy our manna. With each mile, the cans became heavier and heavier. Some of the girls, refusing to give up anything, collapsed under the weight. "Mustn't turn around," you said to yourself. "Don't look back," not even when the crack of the rifle came, finishing anyone who had fallen.

We began dropping parts of our loads. A can at a time. Some girls stopped to pick up discarded marmalade. The crack of the rifle. Don't look back.

The misery of our hunger was compounded by having food in our arms with no way to taste it, with having to throw it away to survive, with having to push on.

The guards mocked and laughed at us. The food was a mirage for us, a game and amusement for them. Our exodus was Sodom and Gomorrah, don't look back.

We marched for two days. Each hour meant a new blister rubbed rough by our wooden shoes. It meant more hunger and more thirst. We each carried a little ceramic water pot, tied around our waist. But the Germans wouldn't let us fill them. We walked with no food and no water.

Occasionally we did stop. It was to let the guards rest or eat while we waited. Once the stop came on the top of a steep hill. As we were sitting down, I saw a creek down the incline. I was gone immediately, scrambling to fetch some of that water. There was no time for Margaret to protest or try to talk sense into me. I had seen the water. I had moved.

A guard saw my scramble. He raised his rifle and fired. The bullet came so close to my wrist that I felt its rush. Before he had time to get off another shot, I was back up the hill and with the rest of the girls. I guess the guard lost interest or was eager to get to his lunch. Nothing else happened, and I had water for Margaret, my cousins, and a few other girls near us.

The only other times we stopped were when planes came roaring down. Our guards dived into ditches or undergrowth. We had to pitch ourselves face down in the road. The planes came down, but the Allied pilots saw that we were *haftlinge*, prisoners, by what we were wearing, and swooped up without firing.

Dundanga, Latvia.

We had shelter, at last. There were many transports in the Lager there, passing quickly through as selections were made and those selected transported out. It was a shipping depot for human goods.

"Margaret, look, it is Eichmann. He is making the selection today."

The specter of death had caught up with us again. It could only mean one thing: We would be dead before the day was over. How many times could we escape death? Some of the women, not in our transport, who had been left in Riga, were evacuated onto a ship. The ship sank and, locked in the hold, they were all killed. It could have been us. There was no reason it wasn't.

Eichmann was going down the rows. For the first time since Auschwitz, the five hundred, fewer now that some had evoked the rifle's crack on the road, were to be separated and regrouped in different transports of five hundred. Eichmann was dividing our group in four sections. He was dividing our lines of five. It could mean that my cousins, sister, and I would no longer be together. We had vowed that somehow we would not be separated, and Eichmann was about to break that vow.

Kato was sent to the first section. That would have to be the group we all went to. Eichmann moved on. Irene took a running step to her sister. Then Margaret moved and made the section. No one had noticed. I was left. I had been the first one, closest to Eichmann and the table of *Aufseherinnen*, female soldiers who acted as overseers. The others had been behind me, so I had shielded their movements. It was now my turn. Eichmann passed me and pointed to where I was to go. It was not Irene's group. I would be all alone without the support of the others. I would never make it alone.

Eichmann, for just long enough, turned away to say something to one of the *Aufseherinnen*. I could see the desperate look on Margaret's face, and that more than anything else made me move. I leaped off the line and dissolved into their group. I was safe.

For each victory there was always a bigger defeat. The little solace we garnered in being together, in having foiled the German system in some small way, was quickly drowned in the despair of our next destination. When the train stopped our newly assembled transport of five hundred was at the Stuttgart concentration camp. Teeming with bone-thin unhuman people, crowded beyond endurance, it was another descent into hell.

"This is it, Margaret. There will be no other stop. This is where we die."

Margaret would not allow it. She was again pacifier and the voice of encouragement.

"Lily, we've come this far. Why would they have brought us here to kill us? Why didn't they kill us in Dundanga or Riga?"

"Why do they do anything?"

We were led into shower rooms and told to clean. It was water and not gas that ran over us.

The showers were an exercise in futility. How could we stay clean when the next few hours were spent sitting in the searing sun, in a dusty yard, with transport after transport moving in and out, stirring up the dust, an endless landscape of gray humanity. Some of those transports were marked for death; others were sent to work. We sat and waited. Which way would we go?

There was no real pattern to who got sent where. The German organization was crumbling, although it seemed as powerful as ever to us and just as unpredictable.

We were remembered. Another inspection. For all our hardships, lack of food, and continual overwork, we were still in relatively good shape. We were young, and we were somehow holding up. We looked as if there was still work left in us. The Germans needed workers—they needed workers desperately.

We were passed. We would help the German Fatherland stave off its inevitable defeat.

20

Leipzig.

In another time, under other circumstances, the man who faced us would have been unassuming, nonthreatening, some-one you wouldn't remember after sitting next to him for five hours on a train. He was too short to be imposing, maybe five feet, eight inches at most, neither slight nor brawny, with a middle-aged softness and a voice that resonated reason and sanity.

Yet as he addressed us, all we could feel was dreadful awe. He wore the uniform of the SS. He was the incarnation of all we had suffered since leaving Tolcsva, the misery, abom-ination, and filth. It was almost impossible to hear his words while concentrating on his uniform.

Besides, what he was saying made no sense, not even after Ica, our block leader, translated it. Never before had a com-mandant bothered to address us. We were so much flotsam to be washed away with a flick of the head. That's what we were used to. But now here was this man, speaking in that reasonable tone, explaining our duties.

"You've been brought here to work. We make planes here, and each step is important and must be done properly. You will help in the assembly. If you do your work, you will be treated fairly. You will be given regular portions and enough to eat. You will get more clothes, warm clothes. You will not be beaten or tortured. You will have to work hard, but it will be honorable work, work that you must take pride in. On the other hand, any attempts to escape, or failure to follow your instructions to the letter or to do your share, will be considered sabotage and handled accordingly."

He left.

"Is this a trick, Ica? Did he really say we would be treated fairly and fed properly?"

Ica knew nothing more than we, although we had grown to expect she would.

Back in Dunganga, an officer had asked, "Who here speaks German?" Ica had been one of the few who stepped forward. She was a short, dark-complexioned, aggressive woman I had noticed before because of an accent that gave her away as being from the Carpathians, a region in the same part of Hungary as Tolcsva.

She spoke several languages, but the important one was German. Our captors needed translators. We were no longer going to be pushed around like cattle. We were to be given more complicated orders, which we would have to understand.

Ica and the others who spoke German were made group leaders. Each had to choose twenty-five or thirty girls. We were among the twenty-eight Ica chose. Ica's sister, Sari, was in our group. They were Aniko, a quiet, extremely lonely girl; Blanca and her sister, Charlotte, who was on the verge of giving in to a breakdown; Serenka; and Sereen, the oldest among us. She might have been forty or she might have been fifty. We didn't know because she never spoke. Sereen wasn't mentally retarded or anything. She was totally indifferent. There was no reason for her talk any more, nothing to say. She became our "fifth" in the lines. Maybe because we cousins had so much to say to each other, we didn't need to force ourselves on her.

We were lucky Ica was our block leader. She was tough, and most importantly, she got things done. She wasn't afraid to go up to a guard and ask, "What's going on here? What's to be done?" We trusted Ica.

I'm not sure we would have trusted her, however, if she had described what was waiting for us. It was a dream, a dream emerging in the wake of a nightmare.

Our barracks, in a Lager about half an hour's walk from the factory, had electricity and *two* washrooms! We each had our own bunk, one per person. True, they were narrow and stacked, but they were the softest, most luxurious of beds to us. When our hair began to grow and we looked like women again, they gave us combs and little mirrors, although I wasn't sure I knew that person looking back at me.

And there was medical care—two doctors and our own little hospital room where the girls went when they were sick. One doctor cured me of the terrible boils I contracted from being weakened and not eating properly. They were big, ugly things. I had one in the same spot on each arm and a third on the side of my breast. The doctor made a little cut in each when they started developing. When they became ripe and enormous, and very painful, the doctor cut them out. One returned, worse than ever, on my right arm. She removed it again but this time gave me an injection. Then they were gone for good. We even had medicine.

And we had food. At the beginning of the week, each girl was given her own loaf of bread to be cut into fourteen slices, two for each day. Each day we got coffee with a teaspoon of sugar! At night there was soup, real soup, with potatoes and meat in it. Once a week, as if already there wasn't enough bounty, we got a piece of sausage. It had been so long since we had eaten like this!

The commandant had not lied about the food. He had got us clothes, including coats. I had a brown plaid coat to get me through the frozen winter. Nor had he lied about the work. We worked hard and long, always fourteen hours a day; yet we were treated not much worse than the Italians, who were political prisoners.

The work we did was nothing I could have imagined back in Tolcsva. We were in quite a sizable plant, big and beautiful. Every five girls had a *Meister*, a German supervisor. He watched every move, checked every step, answered all questions. What we were doing was very exacting. One wrong screw could mean a defective plane.

The first day at the factory we were divided into sections, to work on different stages of the assembly line. Some of the girls cut metal. Others inserted nuts and bolts. Some were actually on the final assembly.

Margaret and I were both assigned to air-drill rivets into a motor part. Each motor took hundreds of rivets that had to be an exact size in an exact position. It would take all fourteen hours to complete only three or four.

It never occurred to me to put a hole in the wrong place or make it too big—not that I could have got away with it, for after each motor part was completed we had to take it downstairs to be inspected carefully by another supervisor. I was scrupulous about performing perfectly, not because I was afraid of the penalties for sabotage, but because I had begun to take pride in my work. I wanted my motor to be without flaw because it was my motor, my work. Who would have thought that a little girl from Tolcsva could handle such a thing as an air hammer? I was confident I always made the right size hole with the right size drill. I was confident that the planes with my motors would fly better and faster than any others. I didn't think about contributing to an effort that had brutalized me and done worse to others in my family. The important thing, the only thing, was getting those rivets right.

A security came with the routine and monotony of our existence, even though we never forgot we were prisoners. We couldn't go to the bathroom or the stockroom at the plant unless accompanied by a female soldier. Our Lager was circled by an electric fence, as if the guards walking the picket and the square tower that lit the yard as bright as the sun at night weren't enough. Unlike the Italian prisoners, we were allowed little freedom of movement. We were walked in to work and back between guns, as if we were criminals. There was really no hope in sight. Now, however, I had begun to daydream, walking in the daylight to the factory, looking up at the clouds so beautiful, so blue, so silent. Nothing moved except us. There were no miracles. But now, at least, life had lost its terror; it had become indifferent, like Sereen.

Some days, my thoughts would be jumbled and full of turmoil. I wanted to escape the questions that had pounded at me since I was put in that wagon in Tolcsva. How was this possible? Why were we so helpless? What had we done? What heinous crime had we committed? Some days I couldn't keep the questions from rocking inside me. Why is the sky so calm? Why are the stars still shining? Who are they shining for? What happened to the blood drained from the bodies of tiny babies and innocent children? Who hears the cries of the sick and disturbed, heals the wounds of the tortured, bandages the hopes of the faithful? Who tends the chosen people now?

There were no answers, only intense silence that was tearing me apart. I did not know, when I thought like that, whether to cry or laugh. It was unbearable. If I kept it up I would be like Blanka's sister, Sari, who had edged closer and closer to insanity until one day she threw herself on the floor and began droning, an old Hungarian song, loudly, without end. No one could make her stop. She had to be bound and carried to the hospital room. It was days before she emerged, quiet, withdrawn. We could see that each day she was inching closer to the precipice. It was only a matter of time before she would be over the edge again.

I couldn't do that. I had to keep my sanity. I couldn't let Margaret down. Without me she would have no reason to be strong and to hope. She needed me as I needed her.

After a while, time and monotony calmed my thoughts. I was able to store them in the back of my mind.

Air raids became more frequent and regular after February 1945. Every night, at almost the same time, you could see Leipzig burning off in the distance. If we were in the Lager, we had to go outside and scrunch into a ditch for shelter. We had no fear. Most of our block would peer over the top, to enjoy the sight of the flaming city. We had absolutely no fear of being bombed ourselves. We knew those were our American saviors up in the planes, and we yearned for their arrival and quietly cheered for their hits.

If we were in the factory, we had to gather up our tools

and instruments into long metal boxes. We were supposed to carry the boxes with us into an underground shelter.

"For goodness' sake, Lily," Margaret would hiss at me. "Shove the stuff into a drawer. No one's going to know. Why carry that heavy thing with you?"

She was right. Everyone hid their tools during a raid. I didn't want to. I wanted to carry them with me. I was proud I was so efficient. I was proud I did things correctly and well. Maybe I could have escaped the factory. The *Hauptmeister*, the head supervisor, a tall man with slicked-back Hitler hair, had taken a liking to me. He made a point of saying hello. He had even offered to get me out of the factory if I went away with him. I wouldn't take his offer, and I wouldn't try escaping. For one thing, I couldn't leave Margaret. For another, this was my job. Leaving wouldn't be efficient.

Our routine was upset in March. Things started happening quickly, piling on top of each other randomly and chaotically.

At the end of March, a Lager on the other side of the city had been bombed. Many of the girls had been killed. Those who survived were being brought to our Lager. We would have to double up and share our food with them. When they arrived, we were shocked and frightened, not by the number of them—there were four hundred—but by their yellow skin and hair.

"Jaundice! Jaundice!" was the whisper that flew through the camp. It wasn't, although they looked starved enough to have been suffering some disease. The girls had been working in a gun-powder plant, and the chemicals had colored their skin. We tried to find someone from Tolcsva among them, but there was no one.

We squeezed into the barracks and made do with the food. What else could be done? And we never stopped working. There were day shifts and night shifts. Get those planes off the line and into the air. Save the Third Reich. Would we ever be saved ourselves?

The air raids increased and became heavier. Most of the time we didn't bother going to the shelter. One day our barracks were hit. Kato had been working the night shift and was asleep in her upper bunk. The bomb dropped. Rafters and beams fell on either side of her. Her bunk collapsed. Kato got only the smallest of scratches. A couple of bunks down, two of the new girls were not so lucky.

When our shift returned that evening we were met with the disaster. We knew there'd been a strike. We didn't know who would be alive. Everyone was hysterical. The bombing didn't stop. Incendiary bombs were exploding all over. Close by, far away. The noise and fear were deafening. I would not go into the nearest bathroom. The bodies had been put there. For all the death that had engulfed me, I had yet to look at a corpse. If one was in front of me, I had looked aside. If one was beside me, I looked ahead. I was not going to look at those bodies now.

We were assembled, in our lines of five, by the commandant's assistant.

"Get sleep tonight," Ica translated. "You will be leaving in the morning."

Sleep was the last thing we got. This night there was no sitting around, combing our hair and talking of recipes our mothers used to make. There was no sleep, either. Ica had said the commandant had told her that day in his office, when she had gone to receive some orders, that the Americans and Russians were tightening a ring around Leipzig and were only ten miles away. The Germans were getting out while they could.

"There is something else I haven't told you yet," Ica said as we lay waiting for another bomb to find our barracks. "The commandant received a message while I was in his office. It was an order from Himmler."

Ica still wasn't sure if she should tell us, whether what she had overheard would reassure us.

"The order said '*Alle Häftlinge sollen vernichtet werden.*' "

Kill all prisoners. Get rid of the evidence. Final Solution? What Final Solution? Jews? What Jews, where?

"The commandant read the message out loud. He stared at it for a while. Then he tore it into the littlest of pieces and threw it into the fire in his stove. 'No. Not my children,' he said."

At daybreak Sari snapped. She began the Hungarian song again, over and over again, louder than the bombs. There was nothing we could do to stop her.

"The roses are blooming under my window," she shrieked. "The roses are blooming there."

We helped the doctors tie her down. There was no time for anything else; the commandant and his aide had arrived. Quickly we formed our lines of five outside, and at the command we left out sanctuary, with the "roses blooming" blasting behind us.

I saw the aide slip away from the line.

One shot. The roses stopped blooming.

We walked for two weeks, in circles, in no direction at all. Blanka had not stopped crying until she ran out of tears. She would not talk to any of us. She had lost the capacity.

The walking went on and on. If we had no idea where we were going, neither did the commandant. Ica explained that he was going to walk us in circles until we found the Americans. If Germans found us first, we would be shot.

We had little food or water with us, though if we came across a stream, we were allowed to stop and drink. We were also allowed to stop if planes came overhead. "On your bellies!" the guards would command, before diving into the ditches. The planes came low, with machine guns firing, until the numbers of our backs were spotted. Then the firing stopped and the planes left.

After the attacks, we walked some more.

Two weeks.

Then we saw the Jeep. Two men were in it. Two gum-chewing, tousle-haired, farmboy, freckle-faced, GI-Joe American boys.

We were saved.

21

If the two boy soldiers didn't much look like saviors, they weren't sure how to act like them either.

Ica had been the first to spot them. She was walking in the lead with the commandant.

"My God! It's the Americans!" We all started scrambling for a look, as if George Patton were in front of us leading a tank brigade.

There was an immediate transformation in our guards. Suddenly they were no longer the fierce SS. Suddenly they were little frightened men, tearing off the rank insignia from their uniforms, throwing away their guns, getting ready to change roles with us, hoping their captors wouldn't be as harsh with them as they had been with us.

Ica yelled, "They might not know we are *Häftlinge*. They might start shooting. Quickly, someone give me an undershirt."

Several girls ran up. Ica grabbed one of the garments, fastened it on a stick, and started waving it.

"We are liberated!" she cried. "You are here to free us!"

The two Americans were completely taken aback. Women jumping up and down all around, yelling completely unintelligible words. German soldiers throwing down guns, raising their arms in surrender. White-undershirt flags appearing all over.

Order was restored when a couple of the German officers went up to explain in English that they were giving themselves up to the American army and placing these prisoners in its custody. The two GIs began rounding up the Germans.

We stood, wondering what would happen next.

"Where is Charlotte?" Ica wanted to know. "Come quickly." I knew immediately the reason for Ica's urgency. Charlotte spoke English, and there was something very important we had to say to these Americans.

"Sirs . . ." Charlotte was frightened of them, but she was more frightened of Ica, who had pushed her to the Jeep and was nudging her on. "Sirs, we are very anxious to tell you something."

"Why sure, honey," the redheaded one said between snaps of his gum.

"We are *Häftlinge*, prisoners, and that man there was our commandant. We must tell you that you shouldn't harm him. He didn't harm us when he could have. He was good to us. We must talk in his behalf, because he was a very righteous man."

The young soldier looked bothered. He should have been home in Iowa, feeding cows; instead, he was on the road between Leipzig and Wurzen, listening to half-dead girls plead for their captor's safety.

"I'm sorry, honey. I wish there was something I could do. I really do. But I got orders to round up any Germans. I don't try them or nothing. I just round them up. But don't worry. He'll be treated fairly. What you girls got to worry about is where you're going next. Wait here and we'll send someone back to get you."

Then they were gone with the Germans and with our commandant. We never saw him again. We never found out what happened to him. We never knew his name.

We sat down to wait.

We had been liberated.

22

Before Hitler, 650,000 Jews lived in Hungary. The Nazis killed 450,000 of them.

23

I really don't remember how long we sat there. My mind was not functioning. I saw nothing, felt, smelled, heard nothing. Eventually, as the soldier had promised, someone came back to fetch us. The Allies had begun setting up the mechanism and bureaucracy to deal with the thousands and thousands of displaced persons. We had gone from prisoner to displaced person. When would we revert to being Lily and Margaret Gluck?

Our escort was taking us to a confiscated house in Wurzen being used as a rescue shelter. We walked to town. It wasn't very far. On the way I discovered a piece of honeycomb by the side of the road. Our luck certainly had changed.

As we munched on it, I said, "Maybe from here on life will be sweeter."

The Americans were very solicitous and caring. They ensconced us in the big old house. They fed us, and when many of the girls got sick from eating too much too fast, they treated us and counseled us on the importance of eating a normal, healthy diet.

"Your days of hunger are over," they assured us. "You

don't have to eat everything at once. There will be more food."

The Americans provided us with food, but sometimes we ran out between deliveries. All we had to do was go to some nearby store and demand what we needed. The city was in disorder, people panicked, homes bombed, businesses abandoned. No storekeeper dared protest when we walked in and said, "We have just been liberated from the concentration camp and we want bread." They always gave us whatever we wanted.

They were a frightened people. They were afraid we'd loot and kill if they didn't comply. Of course, we had no such intentions and were too weak to have done much of anything even if we had. We wanted food, that was all. We had wanted food for so long.

We were in Wurzen for a month, mostly lying about and sleeping. We needed the time to allow apathy to drain out and the acceptance that the worst of our ordeal was over to flow in.

It was a month of suspended animation. We waited to see what would happen next. We hadn't the strength to make anything happen ourselves. We needed the time to reestablish ourselves to ourselves as humans, not objects.

Soon the Red Cross moved in. They faced an awesome task, and the first step was always getting people registered and handing out identification papers. The second step was trying to locate any living relatives. Some of the girls were lucky. Cousins, brothers, fathers, and mothers were found. Most were not.

Margaret and I waited. No one came.

The Americans pulled out, and with them went tranquillity.

Wurzen was on the demarcation line separating the giant armies of the United States and the Union of Soviet Socialist Republics.

The Russians moved in.

They were wild men, fighting, drinking, cursing, and carrying on. They were the victors, and it didn't matter to them that we had been the victims. They saw no difference between us and the Germans.

They were the victors, and they wanted the spoils of war. They wanted women. They wanted us.

We fell back on guile and wits to keep from being raped and shot as was happening to so many women in Wurzen.

One night the inevitable occurred. A mob of drunken soldiers forced its way into our sanctuary. Ica, ever resourceful, had anticipated they might, sooner or later. She had made plans that she quickly put into effect.

"Quick, into the large room upstairs," she ordered us. "Bandage your throats with rags or anything you can lay your hands on. Put kerchiefs on your heads and get into bed. You've just been quarantined."

Before going down to confront the intruders, she hung a Sick Room sign on the outside doorknob.

Intoxicated and boisterous, the Soviets were searching the rooms, refusing to believe Ica's explanation, in Russian, that they had best leave, that we were suffering from a highly contagious, deadly disease. Her explanation did give them pause. Still they wouldn't leave. Ica sat up all night with the officers, conjoling them into leaving. It was daybreak before they did.

Margaret, Kato, Irene, and I decided it was time for us to leave too.

24

We had no money. You don't need money in chaos. The four of us simply boarded a train for Budapest, and that was that. No conductor asked for tickets or threatened to throw us off. Being there and occupying space was tantamount to having a ticket.

The cars were filled by the time we reached Vienna. We had to stand outside on the steps, with the wind slashing at our faces, blowing engine sparks into our eyes, almost blinding us. It didn't matter. We were going back to our Homeland.

It took a full twenty-four hours to reach Keleti Pàlyaudvar station in Budapest.

The wind was howling fiercely, contributing to the strange feelings we were all experiencing. Was this really home? What were we doing here? Why had we returned? Was this Budapest at all?

It was a very different city than the one we had left. Budapest, safe from so much of the war, had been bombed heavily. The few landmarks I remembered from my trips as a child had disappeared.

We had made Budapest our destination because of the faint possibility that Irene and Kato's brother, Miklos, who had been living in the city, might have survived by losing himself in its vastness. It was a possibility, and possibility was the only hope.

We boarded the Villamos streetcar—some things never change—and headed for his old address. It was foolish to think he might be there still. But we had to start somewhere.

He wasn't there. Nothing was there. The building had been bombed into rubble. There wasn't even anyone to ask. The whole block was leveled.

What now? We were four desperate girls, looking for someplace to rest, some small haven to sort out things.

We walked, trying to find someone in the neighborhood who might know of Miklos. Nothing. No one. It was futile. We could have been walking in any city in the world—London, Prague, Chicago. Finally one of the people we stopped told us of an emergency office that had been set up to aid refugees and displaced persons.

There was mayhem at that office, hundreds of people looking for thousands of friends and relatives., There were hundreds and hundreds of names of people and where they were staying listed—including Miklos's! He was alive! And there was an address for him. At last something good.

How do you describe such a reunion? We were apprehensive as we hurried through the streets past all the Russian soldiers. Were we about to be disappointed still again? What if Miklos had moved? What if this was the wrong address? What if he had got sick? What if . . . ?

Miklos opened the door. He had changed very little, a vision from the past, a complete, whole person who showed no signs of ordeal. He couldn't believe we were alive. We were unreal to him. He almost fainted, and we were speechless.

Miklos had survived using false papers and hiding with a Gentile family his parents had known. Now he was living in a tiny one-room apartment that he said would be ours, too.

Miklos was very good to us. He got us decent clothing so we could discard our Auschwitz and factory uniforms. (We kept our coats. Miklos was not made of money, after all.) He wouldn't let us stay anywhere except his apartment. He treated us all like sisters, and he made sure we had plenty of good food.

We could not eat enough, for how could we be sure there would be more food tomorrow, or ever again? We ate and ate until our stomachs could take no more. Then we surreptitiously slipped leftover rolls into our pockets and took them away from the table. We had to be sure that there would be something for us in the middle of the night, the next morning. The fear of hunger haunted us. We could not accept that we were free.

We put the rolls next to our pillows. For security.

We had been in Budapest several days, four girls sharing the small apartment, putting sofa cushions on the floor at night, Miklos sleeping at a friend's.

It was evening when Margaret said without preface, "Lily, it's time we left."

I knew she was right. Miklos was wonderful, but we couldn't impose much longer. It would be hard leaving Kato and Irene after all we had seen together and all we had done.

We had to leave. There was something we had to do, no matter how painful and frightening. We couldn't put it off any longer.

We had to return to Tolcsva.

25

Miklos begged us not to go.

"I'll find another apartment, a larger one we can all share. Don't go. We must stay together. We must be a family."

Margaret and I didn't want to go. We were emotional invalids. We had too few inner resources, too little strength to handle what we might find in Tolcsva—or worse, what we might not find. We were not entirely ready to know the truth—who was left in our family and who was not. Yet we had to pull ourselves together and muster the strength. We had endured the other agonies. We would survive this one too.

Miklos knew. He knew that there would be nobody in Tolcsva, that no one was waiting for us there. He pleaded to hold us back, to spare ourselves this last blow. It was no use. We had to go, and there was no sense putting it off.

When he saw there was no dissuading us, Miklos gave us the little money he had and offered to take us to the train station. There was no point. Margaret and I set out alone.

26

The road looked the same. There were the baron's lands, the houses of his workers, even the storks on the roofs.

We were different, and that made the road painful. I had walked it so many times with my father. I had traveled it with my mother on the way to the *yahrzeits*, memorials for the dead, in Olaszliska. It was the road that took us to the ghetto. Its three kilometers stretched into a lifetime that day.

Margaret and I silently trudged along, both too immersed in our thoughts and memories to say much of anything.

It was a hot July day, and all around us people were doing what had been done for centuries on hot July days—they were working in the fields, in the yards, feeding cattle, washing clothes.

The normality of it all turned me, the pessimist in the camps, into an optimistic idiot. I kept expecting to see Anyuka at the next rise, Apuka around the next bend, Icu and Ernoke running to greet us.

As we came over the last hill, we saw Tolcsva below, its spires and roofs off in the sunlight. It didn't seem so very big any more. It really was a small village.

Izraelita templom. Tolcsva

The synagogue in Tolcsva.

The sign at the Greek Orthodox chuch read, as it always had, WELCOME. PEACE BE WITH YOU.

Peace. What's that? I wondered.

We passed the lumberyard. Men we had known all our lives were busy sawing and packing wood as usual. We passed the now-empty synagogue. Stores were open. There were people in them and in the street. They were people we had seen so many times in the past. They were people who knew Anyuka and Apuka, Ernoke and Icu. They were people who remembered.

They said nothing.

Silence.

Children, Gentile children, were going in and out of houses in which our Jewish playmates had once lived.

It was all the same and all very wrong.

"Let's go to Szalancy's house before going to ours," I said to Margaret. Szalancy had been more than Apuka's caretaker; he had been a friend, a fellow veteran.

It was late afternoon by the time we found Szalancy working in the fields.

"Lily, Margaret. Hello. How are you? Where have you been? And your father, how has he been?"

Was Szalancy kidding? Was this some kind of sadistic joke? We had been gone for more than a year, torn out of town against our will, like so many cattle carted away, and Szalancy was greeting us as if we had come back from a day trip to Sátoraljaújhely.

"We've been on vacation," I said bitterly. "An extended vacation."

He recoiled and said nothing.

The three of us went to our house.

From the outside it looked as it always had—warm and comforting, secure and safe.

Inside, the house was very different. It was no longer the house of my grandfather, where we had been born and taught to love our neighbor and fellowman. It was no longer the house that had belonged to the Gluck family for generations, the house from which my father and his brothers had left to fight World War I in defense of our country. It was some other house, beyond recognition. The floors had been dug up. The furniture was all but gone. Walls were smeared with mud swastikas, doors smashed and left dangling from their hinges. It was a shell, hardly a hint of where we had once been happy. This couldn't be the house where Apuka had thought life began and ended.

We had no place else left to go. Tolcsva, we thought, was our last stop. Szalancy left us to our misery.

Margaret and I lay down in the dirt and slept.

The next day we walked through a village of blind people. No one saw us. No one met our eyes. They hurried about their business, perhaps a bit more solemnly than usual. These after all were the same people who had swooped into our house and taken our possessions. Had moved into our houses as soon as we had been forced out. Had tilled our land when our hoes were taken away. Had laughed at our plight when we left for the ghetto.

Suddenly a flash of color caught my eye. It was my little tennis-racquet dress, my favorite, the one Anyuka wouldn't let me take to the ghetto. It was being worn by someone else. Margaret saw it too. We could do nothing—we were too stunned.

Then I said, "Margaret, I should have a gun. I should start shooting it right here, right away."

"You couldn't shoot it even if you had one. It's not in you to harm another person."

She was right.

"I'll tell you one thing," I said. "I'm going to take back all that was ours. I'm going to rip things right from their arms and their houses. You wait and see."

What I couldn't get back were the people who were missing. *Where is everyone?* I wondered.

Where is our teacher, Bacsi Lukacs, whom we so respected? Where is Doctor Klein, the man who sewed you townspeople after your brawls and saved your lives? Where is Klein the sheet-metal worker who fixed and patched your pots and pans? Green, the baker of the delicious bread? Wrubel, the best dressmaker in town? His son and twelve grandchildren? Who sews the cloth for you now? Where is the shammes, *the caretaker of the synagogue, who walked the streets collecting pennies for the poor and announcing the sad news of someone's death? Who will announce his death now? Where is the envied lawyer Adonyi Pista? The despised old crazy bachelor you used to corner and taunt?*

Who's fixing the town's watches now? Who's cleaning the marketplace? Who is saving your houses now that Fule, the fireman, the only one who could chop a hole in a roof to stop a blaze from spreading, has disappeared?

Where is Apuka, the man you said you admired so much? He was your buddy, the man with whom you had a shot of whiskey or a glass of wine now and then when you wanted to reminisce about old times and the war.

Where are they? What did you do with them? Is nobody

missed? And why did you vandalize the grave of my grand-father? What could you possibly have gained by that?

Life was going on in Tolcsva with no apologies, compassion, or answers. The remains of Tolcsva were living in peace. I had grown up in that village, and I lived to see it bury its guilt with the rest of the world. We had been expendable, so we were trashed.

If only I had had a gun!

We had to live.

The money Miklos had given us ran out soon. In Tolcsva, there was no going into shops and taking what we wanted. The specter of a disapproving mother was over our shoulders. We did have to live, though.

Szalancy had come by to help us look for the "treasure" urn Apuka had buried before we left for the ghetto, those few jewels and trinkets. I was sure I remembered where he had put them. Many holes and hours later they were still not found.

We had nothing. No resources except ourselves.

A couple of days later, I went to Szalancy.

"You must help us," I told him. "I don't want to take anything from you, but I have no choice. My cousin Miklos told us that fresh food is needed in Budapest. If you will give me some of your grape jelly—as Anyuka used to give you some of ours—I'll take it to the city and sell it. That way Margaret and I can live."

"Of course I will, but why don't you and your sister go to your relatives in Budapest? They will help you and make things easier."

He didn't need an answer. He could see it in the set of my jaw and the sorrow-filled anger in my eyes

We had to wait, in Tolcsva. We had to give Anyuka and Apuka, Icu and Ernoke time to join us. We couldn't leave.

So I began traveling to the city. Miklos put me in touch with some middlemen, who gratefully took the jelly and paid me well, sometimes with money, sometimes with clothing or food.

It was tiring and worth it. I was able to get Margaret new shoes, and we were never hungry. It was also nerve trying. Russian soldiers were everywhere and as unpredictable as ever. They were the conquerors and were growing accustomed to taking what they wanted.

When the train stopped at Szerencs, a Russian soldier got on. I watched him move up the aisle and wished I were invisible. I knew he was coming to me. He was going to sit down next to me.

He did and then started speaking, in Russian. Why he thought a young girl on a train in Hungary would speak Russian or was Russian, I don't know. He did.

"I'm sorry. I speak very little Russian," I tried to explain. "I'm Hungarian."

He couldn't understand or didn't want to and he was getting angry. He obviously didn't believe I couldn't understand him. Desperately I kept talking.

"I'm returning to my sister . . . after selling jelly in Budapest . . . for clothing. Please, I'm working to get a few *pengos*, a few coins, to live on. . . . We got back from a camp only recently. . . . We don't know where our parents are. . . . Please leave me alone. . . ."

In a fury, the soldier grabbed my knapsack and threw it out the window. It was my entire wealth in the world. Without it, Margaret and I would have nothing. When the train started to move, the soldier looked away for a second. Long enough. I couldn't stay there. I had to retrieve my knapsack. I ran up the aisle and threw myself off the speed-gaining train.

I should have been killed or crippled. Instead, I bruised my ankle. I waited all night for another train. After that I shivered every time I saw a Russian. My youth and rosy cheeks had become a liability.

27

And so we waited. Each day robbed us of little more hope and chipped away at the likelihood that anyone was returning.

Our presence, like our arrival, was met with continued silence from the rest of Tolcsva. Sometimes I asked people what they thought had happened to us. Why hadn't they stopped it? Refused to use their wagons? Refused to let us be taken? My answer was incomprehension. Collective amnesia had infested everyone. What ever was this wild and strange girl asking them? What did she want from them?

Summer into autumn.

A school friend, Zsuzsi, bald and gray pallored, showed up one day. We joined forces, moved into her old house because it was in better condition than ours. She ate what we ate. We all made do.

Autumn into winter.

November 1945. A knock. It was a boy from the post office with a telegram from the Red Cross.

YOUR BROTHER ICU IS ALIVE IN PARIS.

Seven incredible, marvelous words, the sweetest of sweet words that we had dreamed of reading someday, were now before us.

"Thank God! Someone is alive!"

We were no longer alone.

There was no question we were going to Paris and no thought of how. We just would. There was nothing for us in Tolcsva. The sooner we left the better.

That proved to be a month.

There were things to be done, more word from Icu to be received.

The latter arrived in the form of two letters. Icu was recuperating, but he was all right.

We had a little money saved by then.

I went to Budapest and spent some of it on cloth. I had a fur-lined coat made for Margaret. For me, I made a pair of pants and an unlined jacket. My labor-camp coat would have to do for a bit longer. We packed the knapsack and tied up a blanket with the meager belongings we had accumulated. There were no goodbys other than to Zsuzsi. We were ready to go.

It was only then that it hit us. Somehow we had to make our way across Russian-held territory and half the war tatters of Europe. It wasn't going to be easy. There was no point being overwhelmed by what lay ahead. We would have to take one step at a time and not think about all the others that were to follow. The first step was getting out of Hungary.

We left Tolcsva with no regrets and little feeling. I worried some about Zsuzsi. Would she be able to fend for herself? She had become stronger, and I could only wish she would make it. We could do no more for her. We had to reach Icu.

In Budapest, Miklos took us to a Zionist organization that arranged for people to get to Palestine. The Russians didn't want anyone to leave, so the group had to spirit people out of the communist zone. It was dangerous.

I went to the organization's little one-room office, with its scarred desk. I told the contact there that my sister and I wished to live in Israel. It was a necessary lie.

We were accepted. Meet at a certain house on a certain night and we would be given further instructions. Be prepared to travel light, fast, and on foot.

The night came and with it more leavetaking. It was very difficult. Would we ever see our beloved Kato and Irene again? And Miklos? It was best to stay focused on Icu and the pleasure that awaited us.

There were thirty-five of us leaving that night. Thirty-five strangers who quickly became a loyal, cohesive band. Our leaders were two Polish boys who had taken the trip many times before. They knew where the Russians would be. They knew which roads to take and which rocks to hide behind.

It was a terror-filled, exhausting trip. From the plains we had to cross the Trans Danubian Central Mountains, or Carpathians, to reach Austria. There were easier routes, but not if we wanted to elude the Russians.

As it was, their patrols were everywhere. When we stumbled on one, we immediately flattened ourselves to the ground as the Polish boys had instructed and waited for the flashing lights to move on and dim.

The miles, rocks, and scrambling were especially hard on Margaret. The new shoes I had bought her with some of my first jelly money were carving blisters into her feet. Soon it was necessary for some of the boys and me to take turns dragging her along. Her pain was intense. By the first morning her foot was swollen and red with infection. There was no stopping until we reached the American zone. Margaret had to suffer until we got there.

But all things end, and this trip ended in Vienna.

We moved into a house there that the organization used as a waystop. As the others rested I got Margaret to a doctor who treated her foot and gave her some kind of shot. Still more of our preciously small hoard of money was gone.

It took a full week for Margaret to recover. That gave me an excuse to tell the Polish boys and the others to leave without us. We would go to Paris instead on our own.

We had reached the next step. To get to Paris we would need papers and identification. Even in the postwar confusion, I knew we would not get far alone without them. I started asking around and pestering. Where should I go for papers? The only possibility seemed to lie with an organization set up by several countries, including the United States, to help returning soldiers get resettled. It was close enough. The organization would have to do.

I marched myself over and demanded to see someone. I was shunted off to an American officer who spoke German.

I told him my problem.

"I'm sorry—there's nothing I can do for you. I would suggest you return to Hungary and wait for your brother to get to you."

"We can't do that. He's recuperating and we don't know how long that will take."

"Well, all I can tell you is you can't travel without papers, and I don't issue them."

"You're an American, aren't you?" I asked indignantly. "And you're an officer. Surely you can give me something. My sister and I are going to Paris whether you do or not, so why don't you help us?"

"How can I? I'm not authorized. Everything is in shambles, and no one is equipped to issue papers. Trying to get to

Paris without them is stupid and impossible. You'll end up in some pokey someplace."

And so it went. The officer refusing, me insisting, until he capitulated.

"Okay, okay, okay. What I will do for you is this: I will give you a letter. If you get stopped, show it. Maybe it will help."

I had won. What more did I need than a letter from an American officer? What could be more official?

Of course, I had no idea what was in the letter. I didn't read English. Later I was to find out that all it said was that I was trying to reach my brother in Paris and any help would be appreciated. Nothing more. I, however, decided the letter stated that my brother was in the American army and that I had to be helped by order of General Dwight David Eisenhower or the president or some such person.

That paper became the most precious thing I had ever possessed. It was my talisman, my passport to Icu. I wouldn't even let Margaret hold it.

It took most of the rest of our money to get tickets from Vienna to Munich, where we had to change trains. With the last of our hoard, we went to buy tickets there, to continue. The ticket agent refused to sell me any.

"Listen, kid," he said, "I don't know how you got this far, but if you want to go any further, you're going to have to show me a passport."

"This official American-army letter is instead of a passport."

"Says who? I don't want to see any letter. Look, it's in English, anyway. I can't read that. Either you show me passports or get off the line."

Margaret pulled me away before I could continue the argument.

"Lily, you're going to get us both arrested. What are we going to do now?"

"Let's go out to the tracks. Maybe we can sneak onto a train."

There was actually a train there, being boarded.

"Where's that train going," I asked a maintenance man.

"It's an American troop train," he said. "It's for American soldiers on their way home. It should be pulling out any minute now for Paris."

Paris.

Perfect. "We're going, too."

"But you can't, Fräulein," he protested. "It's only for soldiers. You can't buy a ticket for that train."

"Then we'll go without a ticket," I said, and pushed poor Margaret up the steps before we could be stopped.

By chance we had boarded a sleeping-compartment car.

"This is beautiful," I said. "Come on. Let's pick a room and get settled. We're going to ride in style."

Margaret looked dubious, but what could she do? If I decreed we were riding in style, that's how we were riding.

She looked more than a little relieved when the train got underway. Surely then next stop would be Icu.

There was a lot of milling about and movement in the corridor as tardy arrivals looked for their assigned places. Our door opened, and there stood several officers, mouths agape. They hadn't, after all, been expecting to see two young female civilians on a military transport. And they especially had not been expecting to find them sitting in their compartment.

Tickets were in their hands, which they kept checking against the number on the door. No doubt about it, this was their room. They started asking us questions, and even though

I could figure out what they were saying, I played dumb. We weren't budging. They called for reinforcements in the uniform of a conductor.

"What language do you speak?" he asked in German.

No answer.

He rattled off a list of possibilities. English? Russian? Français?

I acted as if I had suddenly understood.

"Romanian," I said, for some inexplicable reason. Someone was quickly dispatched to comb the train in search for anyone who spoke Romanian. It took a while until someone was found.

I was asked what I was doing there, in Romanian.

Nope, don't understand, I indicated. "Czechoslovakian," I said. Now it was off in search of someone who spoke Czech. All fine with me. The longer they took, the less likely it was they'd put us off. It would take too long to get the train back to Munich. Margaret sat, a petrified column. Surely, she thought, Lily had gone mad.

This time, a young private was brought back. He sat very close to me and in German whispered so the others couldn't hear, "Listen—you are Jewish, aren't you? Don't be frightened —so am I. Nothing is going to happen to you, but you have to get out of this compartment. It belongs to those captains, and they aren't taking too kindly to giving it up to go back and sit with the enlisted men. So now, you come along with me to third class, and we'll sit back there until we all get to Paris. Okay?"

He seemed a trustworthy sort. And he was Jewish. When we got back to the crowded third-class section, Margaret refused to enter the car. She was scared.

"We can't go in there—not with all those soldiers," she hissed. "They will rape us for sure."

"Margaret, don't be silly. They're not Russians. They're American boys. Come on."

The private got us situated, then went off to get food from the dining car. We sat up all night talking—the war and Tolcsva, our family and his. In the morning, we pulled into the elaborately beautiful Gare Saint-Lazare, one of Paris's railroad stations.

There was no trouble getting off the train. No one thought to stop us walking through the gates with all those soldiers.

Our private was worried. We were so young. We didn't speak French. We were looking for our brother who could be at either of two addresses or anywhere else. The private couldn't stay to help us. He wanted to but was shipping out immediately. What he could do was tuck a hundred francs into my hand and tell us to take care.

No place we had ever been prepared us for Paris. It was elegant, fashionable, alive. The war and its aftermath were lost in its spirit. All we could do was gape and gawk through the window of the little café in which we chose to have our first meal. It was there we discovered that one hundred francs go very quickly in Paris. We would have to find Icu soon, if not immediately.

We had to make a choice—which address to try first. It seemed reasonable to me that we go to the place from which the letter that arrived last had been sent. It was a place called Ambloa. We had no idea where this Ambloa was and the idea of using a phone to find out if Icu was there never occurred to us. I stopped a gendarme. He was very patient while I pointed and gesticulated to try and make him understand what I wanted to know. It was then his turn to gesture,

and soon we realized that we would have to go to some other station to get to Ambloa. He sensed that this would be no easy task for us, so instead of pointing us on our way, he took me by the hand, into the Metro and to the station. I had to pull Margaret along. It was beyond reason, but she thought we were back in Germany before liberation. She thought the gendarme was arresting us.

The train ride to Ambloa took several hours. Through the good graces of the policeman we got on free. In the evening we arrived at a lonely station. One sole person there got it across to us which direction to walk to the address we wanted. It was four or five miles. It didn't matter. We would have walked five times that to get to Icu that night.

At the address a lovely young girl answered the door.

I pulled out a photo Icu had sent. "We are looking for our brother, Icu Gluck. Here he is in the picture. May we see him now, please?"

"Oh no," she said. "You are too late. No. No. I didn't mean that. Your brother didn't die. He was among those that left for Taverny."

It couldn't be. We had been sure we were close to our brother. Would we never be allowed to meet?

The girl continued, "You will have to go all the way back to Paris. You have to catch another train at the Gare du Nord. It will take you to Taverny. You look exhausted, so I'll arrange for someone to drive you back to the station. I am sorry."

We spent the night in the waiting room on the blanket we had brought from Tolcsva.

In the morning we caught the first train to Paris. We had no money. The ticket-control man had tried to stop us at the gate before boarding. I told him we were going to Paris, that we didn't have any money, and there was nothing I could do about that.

"You'll be put off at the next big station," he said, "and then it will be off to jail."

"Fine. That's not my worry. At least we'll be fed there."

I pushed my way past him with Margaret in tow and jumped on the train.

We arrived in Paris without incident and without tickets.

For some reason the city didn't seem as strange and alien as it had the day before. I didn't hesitate to approach another gendarme, and again he took us by Metro to the station we needed.

As we were waiting for the train, I noticed a young boy wearing a beret. Don't ask me why, but I thought he might be one of the boys from the orphanage in Taverny. He looked like us; he looked as if he could have been in Icu's picture.

"Excuse me—I have a picture of my brother here. Would you happen to recognize him? He's that one, there."

He hardly glanced at it.

"Why, sure, I know him. That's Icu. He's in Taverny, with the rest of us."

We were almost home.

28

It was brisk that November day we walked in the sunlight under tall green pines on our way to the castle turned orphanage at Taverny. Fogel, for that was the name of the bereted boy at the station, told us a little about the place and its inhabitants.

It was part of an Ouvres Secures aux Enfants (Organization for Protection of Children, or OSE) operation to give children of the Holocaust a chance to mend and readjust. It was also a place where these displaced and battered children and young men could pick up some skills and learning to prepare them for the rest of their lives.

Practically all the boys in this particular group, except for Icu, were survivors of Buchenwald. (Icu had been sent from a Red Cross hospital to join this group.) It started out with a thousand young men and boys discovered by the liberating American army and a Doctor Ravel, an American, who followed the army hoping to do something for the survivors. In Barracks 66, Buchenwald, he found those boys, all Hungarian, except for twenty very young Polish boys, who had been hidden and kept alive with sugar cubes and water.

"They can't stay here," Doctor Ravel announced. "If they stay here, in their rundown condition, they will all perish."

He sent telegrams to the OSE offices in Geneva, Paris, and London: WE HAVE DISCOVERED A GROUP OF ONE THOUSAND CHILDREN. THEY MUST BE EVACUATED IMMEDIATELY. It took four weeks to get the things set up for the boys to be moved to France.

The OSE found an empty castle in Ecouis, one that had been used as a sanatorium. It was to be reequipped completely for the boys. In the cross and flurry of telegrams and letters a gross misundertsanding occurred. The boys were primarily between the ages of sixteen and twenty-four. Ecouis was waiting for infants and toddlers. Hundreds of cradles and baby beds were brought in. Formula was stocked, pediatric nurses hired.

The arrival of the not-so-tiny charges caused bedlam. Doctor Ravel had got the boys to trust him and talked them into leaving the few possessions they had foraged after liberation only by promising them the French would give them ten times as many things that were ten times as good.

The train trip to Ecouis had been one of elation and high spirits. The boys jumped off at every station, to smell the flowers and look at the blossoms, just to prove that they were indeed liberated and free. The train master had been told to let them do as they pleased. With all the ons and offs, the trip stretched on for days.

Ecouis came as a confusing shock. Where were the promised things? What were these baby beds? The boys were sure they had been tricked and betrayed.

There wasn't even proper food for them. The staff hurriedly scrambled to find some cheese for the first meal. A rumor quickly buzzed through the group: "Don't eat the cheese. It's poison."

The boys had survived the Germans, to be finished off by the French.

It took a lot of fast talking and more promises to settle the crisis.

The following days were spent settling in and exploring, after which the large, unwieldy group began organizing. Boys from the same village banded together, older with younger. Another problem developed with the organization. Some of the boys did not want to eat *traif*, nonkosher food. They wanted to be separate from the nonorthodox boys in a place where they could establish a kosher religious atmosphere and live by the traditional rules they followed at home.

To accommodate this, the OSE rented another castle, this time in Ambloa, a wonderful place with a large park and a forest beyond that.

It was idyllic there. Two women—tall, blond, pug-nosed Judith, a German Jew, and dark-haired, pretty Nini, a French Jew—were hired to help Leo Margulies care for the boys.

Mr. Margulies (no one would have thought of calling him Leo) had spent almost a quarter of his life, from 1933 to 1945, in concentration camps. The last four years had been in Buchenwald. He had done the impossible—he had lived. He was the perfect leader for these religious boys, the perfect example to emulate, for despite what had happened to him, his morale had never lowered. He had never denied the existence of his God, despite those years in Buchenwald. He had walked out as profoundly religious as when he entered. And he still believed in humanity. He gave the boys new strength through his own.

Once, in the beginning before the boys really knew Mr.

Margulies, a shipment of clothes arrived and was put in a store room. Some of the boys wanted to go in immediately, to get rid of the despised German uniforms they had been wearing since liberation, the only clothes that had been found for them.

Mr. Margulies stopped them. "I'll take charge of the storage room."

He went in and locked the door so he wouldn't be disturbed. The boys became restive. What was he doing in there for three hours? Was he choosing dream attire for himself with matching shoes? When he got what he wanted, would the boys then be allowed to sift through the leftovers? They were angry and anxious.

Finally Mr. Margulies opened the door. He had picked something out for himself—an old vest and an old black beret. What he had been doing for all that time was sorting the rest of the clothes by size and style.

"Now you can enter, and it will be easier for you to pick what is best for each and every one of you."

While Mr. Margulies gave them strength and faith, Judith and Nini gave them happiness. Little things. For example, when the women realized some of the younger boys had not been Bar Mitzvahed because they turned thirteen in the camp, they organized a party for them. They bought as much candy as the budget could afford and a little present for each of the boys being Bar Mitzvahed. Judith and Nini made it a special day for each of them, like family. Each honoree was given time to reminisce about their lost families and homes and about what they wanted for the future. They played games and laughed, and for a brief time they were able to forget the years of suffering. For a few hours they were innocent children again.

No one wanted to leave Ambloa, but it was too far from Paris, where the boys could get schooling and instruction in trades. Taverny was chosen as a substitute. The OSE was able to get another castle there, Le Château de Vaucelle. The trains ran regularly between Vaucelle station and the Gare du Nord, making it easy to commute. So the move was made.

At the château's gate Margaret and I had to stop for some deep breaths, to gain composure. In minutes we would be seeing our wonderful brother. He was steps away, somewhere beneath the trees in the garden or under the roof of the imposing château. He had no idea we were there.

We went in. Fogel took off in search of Icu.

What would we say to Icu? Would he look the same? Would we recognize him? Had we changed that much?

We were almost at the front door when he came soaring out, arms thrown wide, smiling as I have never seen anyone smile before.

29

After kissing us, crying, hugging us, and making sure we weren't ghosts, Icu took us inside.

I had a chance to study him more closely. The smile was the same, the features recognizable. However, the signature of his nightmare was etched across his face, which was grotesquely swollen. He was missing a front tooth. His feet were swollen as well. He was weak and quickly out of breath. The important thing to us was that he was alive and we were with him. There was something else important to Icu. He had something to tell us, and he wanted to get it over quickly.

It was the story of the last year and a half, his story beyond the train tracks at Auschwitz.

Ernoke had been separated from Apuka and Icu at the tracks, as Anyuka had been taken from us. Icu never saw him again.

Apuka and Icu were put into a work party that was quickly shipped out of Auschwitz. Much as we had been, their party was shuttled from location to location. They were treated even worse than we, with harder work, less food, more beatings, and indiscriminate shootings. Clubbed, starved, worked beyond exhaustion, many died. Others wished they could. Apuka and Icu endured. They couldn't long for death because they couldn't abandon each other. They kept each other going and refused to succumb.

Liberation. They had outlived the Final Solution. They were free.

Icu became very sick. It was as if, with freedom, he let his defenses drop. Both Apuka and he were shipped to a Red Cross hospital in Mulhouse, France.

What happened there shouldn't have happened, and it probably wouldn't have except for the scrambled pandemonium the surrender brought. Icu needed blood. He didn't have a rare type, so it wasn't as if there was no other blood to be had. Still, when Apuka volunteered to donate, the doctor accepted.

Soon afterward, Apuka fell ill himself. Hepatitis. The needle had been dirty. Two weeks later, his body too

My father's grave.

debilitated from the camp experience to put up much resistance to the hepatitis, Apuka died. Disease and a Red
Cross hospital accomplished what Hitler couldn't.

Apuka was buried with military honors in an old Jewish
cemetery on Zilisheim Street, in Mulhouse, under a small tree
and some bushes. He had always liked the shade. His name
was Zoltan Gluck. May he rest in peace, for he wasn't
allowed to live that way.

30

Margaret and I were like the man who came to dinner. We stayed.

At first we were concerned. After all, Taverny was for boys. There were other OSE places for girls. We were afraid we would be sent to one of those. Judy made some calls, and as Icu's sisters, we were allowed to stay.

I started taking French lessons, first with the woman, mademoiselle Mann, who came to the château, and then in Paris. Within three months I could speak well enough to get by nicely—so well, in fact, that the OSE gave me money for further schooling.

In the fall of 1946, I enrolled in classes at the Sorbonne —mathematics, physics, chemistry. I didn't make many friends there. I didn't want to. There was one Romanian boy I talked to between lectures. But mostly, instead of socializing, I would sit by myself in the peace and beauty of the Luxembourg Gardens.

One particular day I was absently feeding pigeons and thinking, so engrossed that I didn't notice the man who sat on the bench with me.

When the bird seed was gone, my revery went with it. It was time to collect my books and get back to class.

A hand took mine.

"Please," the man on the bench said, in halting French, "don't leave yet. Look at me. I know you will remember me. I believe we have seen each other under very different circumstances."

Who was this man? My heart was pounding sickenly fast. I had to flee from this crazy person. Then something about his face caught me. There was something familiar there. I tried to remember. Where?

It was not his features. It was his expression.

I was trembling. Irrationally I asked, "How did you get here? When did you sit down on the bench? There was no one there when I sat down."

"I know. I was walking by and saw you feeding the

My student card at the Sorbonne for 1946–47.

pigeons with the same expression and in the same manner you fed me for those many days."

The tremble was now a shaking.

"Are you Latvian?" I was unable to accept he might be who I thought.

"Yes."

"Were you in Riga?"

"Yes."

"Did you used to reach for a bowl over the latrine fence and take it from a young girl?"

"Yes," he sighed with pleasure.

"Then you are the man I used to give my soup to because I couldn't stand the taste of it."

"Yes."

It was silly, but I was embarrassed. "I am sorry that was the only thing I had to give you."

"Oh no, don't be. I can't tell you how thankful I was for that. You may have saved my life. I'm sure of it. I would have died if I hadn't gotten that extra food just then."

We sat looking at the flowers for a while; then he got up.,

"I may never see you again. I'm leaving tomorrow for New Zealand. I want to get as far away from this continent as I can. Thank you. Good luck and God bless you."

I didn't return to class that day. I spent it aimlessly wandering the city until it was time for the last train to Taverny.

31

Life was pleasant in Taverny. Margaret and I had our own little field house. We ate meals with the boys in the château's great hall. I went to my classes. Margaret went to trade school, where she was taught sewing. Icu studied the Talmud.

We had no real chores around the castle except for keeping our own rooms clean and once in a while helping with cooking or laundry.

It was a comfortable life with good people. Elie Wiesel, the future author, was among those with us.

After a time, our numbers dwindled. Some of the boys went to live with found or distant relatives in other countries. Some went to Palestine. I was content to stay. I liked France. I liked its language—it was all I spoke since I had determined to put Hungary behind me. I was gaining a sense of belonging.

Icu, on the other hand, wanted to leave. He argued that there was no future in France for us. The United States was the land of our opportunities.

He wrote to Aunt Hani, asking her to find us a sponsor. She did, a second cousin of Mother's, who lived in Pennsylvania. Between Judith and Hani our papers were obtained. Since Margaret and I were both under twenty-one, we could

Some of the Taverny boys and Judith. My brother is in the back row, wearing the beret. Judith is in the center, and Fogel, who led us to Taverny, sits in front of her.

emigrate under the children's quota. Even most of those had been filled, so we were technically traveling as children from Czechoslovakia, since that country's emigration allowance had not been reached. Icu had to wait, since he was older. In the meantime he was learning a trade, diamond cutting, that he thought would give him a better chance of obtaining a visa. He traveled to Belgium for the training, crossing the border illegally. He got caught once and spent a week in jail before the judge decided he had been punished enough for this minor crime.

Waiting for visas was hardly unusual. It took years before Mr. Margulies got his. He was one of the last to leave Taverny, and from what Judith later told us, it was a tender departure.

Mr. Margulies had always admired Judith. Right before he was to leave, he invited her to dinner in Paris. He would never have dreamed of doing so before.

He took her to a fine restaurant and ordered the best of the menu.

"After dessert," Judith recounted, "he took out a little box containing a pen and handed it to me. I was pleasantly surprised, and he was proud of his choice. And then he suggested we go to a movie."

They stood in line to see a thoroughly American movie, Kirk Douglas's *The Bad and the Beautiful,* as fine snowflakes were falling. The snow covered branches and little by little blanketed the fences around the trees.

Even in such a serene scene, Mr. Margulies had memories. "This reminds me of Buchenwald at the hour of *Zell Appell* in the wintertime. Sometimes the *Appells* lasted a long time, and very often it snowed. People dropped dead sometimes,

right on the spot. The snow covered them and then everything was white again."

In New York, Mr. Margulies eventually married and had
three sons.

April 1947.

Margaret and I boarded a small U.S. army transport ship,
the U.S.S. *Marina Falcon*. Most of the other passengers were
soldiers returning from their tours of duty. The rest was a
mix of people—businessmen, some French boys and girls, and
us.

It was not your first-class *Queen Mary* crossing. The tiny
ship didn't seem big enough to handle the North Atlantic
storms; its ballasts not big enough for the buffeting by mountains of waves. Water lapped into our cabins. We were
always having lifeboat drills because there was a good chance
the next time wouldn't be a drill.

There was rarely anyone at meals. They were all too sick.
But no rough sea was going to keep Margaret and me from
eating. We didn't miss a meal.

Fourteen days of storm. Only as we came in sight of land
did the rains and winds abate, as if the fairy-tale skyline of
New York City somehow cleared the air. We could see the
Statue of Liberty. As the boat passed the stately welcomer
to the New Life, I took off my brown plaid coat, the one
I had had since the labor camp, and threw it into the water.

"What on earth did you do that for?" one of the French
girls asked.

"We're going to be Americans now," I explained. "We're
going to live in the United States. Here you can get all the
coats you want. Who needed that one?"

Doctor Z. Roth, the husband of my mother's second

cousin, was waiting for us at the dock. He had no trouble picking us out of the crowd coming down the gangplank., We looked exactly like what we were—two young European girls anxious to start anew.

We were going home with him, to Reading, Pennsylvania, until we decided where we wanted to live and what we wanted to do.

It may sound untrue, but I could feel the excitement of the United States enveloping me as soon as I set foot on its soil. Here was that special place where Anyuka had believed goodness resided. It made me giddy. It made me feel fortunate.

With all the required formalities out of the way, Doctor Roth whisked us into his car and onto the highways.

Highways were something far beyond my experience—the speed, the billboards, and most of all, the Howard Johnsons. It was without doubt the most fabulous, beautiful, American place on all the earth—all that food, all that polish, *all those flavors of ice cream!* Howard Johnsons was truly the United States, and butter brickle was truly what it meant to be an American.

32

We stayed in Reading only three days. Our cousins had been kind enough to sponsor us. That was enough. We didn't want to take advantage of their kindness. Besides, there was nothing for us to do in Reading. We wanted to work. Make our living. Be independent. I was nineteen.

Margaret decided at dinner the second night that we would go to Brooklyn, where several of our Taverny boys had already scratched a toehold.

We were lucky. One of them, Menache Klein, was able to arrange for us to stay in a tiny room, on the top floor of a shul, rent free. It was furnished, in a manner of speaking, with two beds and one broken table. Its two windows looked out on an overgrown, debris-prone garden. We shared a kitchen with another couple.

No one had cleaned that room for a long time. We were greeted by dust, cobwebs, and our cohabitants, the bugs in the beds.

"We came all the way to the United States for this?" I asked Margaret, longing for the pristine loveliness of Taverny.

It was depressing and defeating, but by morning tears had

Margaret and me shortly after our arrival in the United States.

Icu

been wiped away. I was young and free, and things would get better.

Menache gave us the address and directions to the United Service for New Americans, in a new building on Chambers Street, in downtown Manhattan.

The service's purpose was to provide monetary help, counseling, and job placement for us displaced, lost people. It was a godsend at first.

Margaret had her sewing. I was totally unskilled. We both took any job that was available—putting tips on umbrellas, working in shoe factories, dress plants, dry-cleaning stores—all temporary positions, fill-ins, until someone with experience came along or someone came back from vacation. If the job called for a floor girl, I didn't care that I didn't know what a floor girl was. I'd volunteer. I'd learn.

At night I took free English courses at Washington Irving High School. In the day I worked. The summer of 1947 was unbearably hot, and it wasn't easy for us. Margaret fainted more than once, and sometimes I wondered if we hadn't entered another bad dream.

It was three months before the isolation and continual fright began to fade as I picked up more and more English.

Life was grueling. If it hadn't been for the free rent, I don't know what we would have done, especially after I refused to return to the service and had to find work on my own.

Cutting the umbilical cord from the service came after I had been dismissed from one job and had gone back to check job listings. There was a new caseworker handling my file, an officious so-and-so who was more interested in exerting his authority than in actually helping me.

He scanned the list of jobs before shaking his head.

"Sorry, there is nothing for you this week. Only this maid's job that requires too much experience and too much heavy work—washing windows, things like that. You're much too young for that."

Was this man crazy? It would be nothing compared to what I had done in the war. I needed that work.

"I can do it," I insisted. "I want that job to make money and support myself so I don't need your help, so I can get a real apartment."

He kept shaking his head in his obnoxiously pompous way. It was too much. I started crying.

"Lily, you're not getting that job. Furthermore, I think you're demonstrating with this scene that you are not adjusting to your life here. I am going to have to get you psychiatric help."

Psychiatric help when all I wanted to do was make something of myself?

"You're the one in need of psychiatric help!" I shouted, and left.

1948 was a much better year for us. Icu arrived. We were able to get another apartment, in the Williamsburg section of Brooklyn on Bedford Avenue, gathering place for new-comers.

Icu, through a friend's recommendation, was hired by a Hebrew publishing house, to work in its prayer-book section. I had got a steady job typing address labels in an office. I taught myself to type well enough to get by, never being afraid to admit when I didn't know how to do something and never being afraid to try to do it anyway.

We were still "greeners," as the more established in the neighborhood called us, although each day we were becoming more and more Americanized. Margaret and Ruthie, my friend from the floor below us, would join other young girls strolling down the avenue. We'd stop to flirt with boys and sometimes let them walk with us. We found ways to entertain ourselves—movies, skating, exploring Manhattan.

One day I received a telephone call. It was from a fellow that Icu had seen in synagogue at Purim, a Hungarian who had arrived in the United States only two months earlier.

"Your brother gave me your number. I would like to meet you. Would Saturday night be all right?"

What was there to lose? Icu had mentioned talking to a good-looking man, and I liked good-looking men.

"Sure. I'm not busy. Come over at seven or seven-thirty. We live at 175 Taylor Street, third floor."

I began having second thoughts about the invitation. What if this guy was a dud? I'd be stuck the whole evening. I enlisted Ruthie's help. She would be visiting when this guy arrived. At least if he was terrible, I could talk to Ruthie.

Saturday. Promptly at seven there was a knock at the door. I opened it and got my first look at Harry Lerner.

It was not an auspicious first date. I had tried to guess where he would take me, what we would do. I had never been on a full-fledged date before. I don't think I would have guessed that we would spend the entire evening, the three of us, talking nothing but politics. Harry was very big on politics—what to do with Japan, how to handle China, reparations, war-crime trials . . . the man never stopped talking and arguing.

By the end of the "date" I couldn't say that I thought much of him. Ruthie was even less charitable.

"What a cheap guy," she said when he finally left. "He didn't even take you out to a movie."

"Maybe he doesn't know what you do over here on a date. He just got off the boat."

So much for that guy, I thought.

The next day Harry surprised me with another call. "What are you doing today?" he asked.

"Well, I was planning to go skating."

"May I come along?"

"Do you like to skate?" I was puzzled. Harry had not struck me as someone who engaged in such frivolous pastimes.

"No," he answered. "But I would like to come along."

So he did.

On Wednesday he called again. I was going to the gym at the YW-YMCA. Could he come, too? Why not?

Wednesdays. Saturdays. Sundays. He got to be a habit, one I liked.

Over the weeks, Harry told me his story.

33

HARRY'S STORY

I was born in 1923 in Kisvárda, Hungary, about 320 kilometers east of Budapest, not far from where Lily was born. It was a town of about fourteen thousand people, of whom some four thousand were Jewish.

It was a special place. The Jewish families had lived there between 50 and 150 years. They were well established in a mixture of trades and professions. There were Jewish doctors, lawyers, large landowners, merchants, tradesmen, scholars, and authors. There were several Jewish law offices, twelve doctors. The six Jewish midwives had delivered 90 percent of the entire town. My family had been in many businesses. We had been cattle and rawhide dealers and feather exporters, and we had dealt with furs. Our neighbors were lumbermen, storekeepers, tradesmen, tailors, cobblers.

I can't really liken it to anywhere else I've ever been. The Jewish community in Kisvárda was stable, solid, and productive. It looked as if my people had been there for a thousand years and would stay forever. There was no sign nor hint that anything could interrupt this community, even though life

Harry's house in Kisvárda.

was difficult there. We worked hard, and it was fulfilling.

People helped their neighbors in Kisvárda. If one needed money, you lent him some, even if it meant borrowing from someone else to get it. You then borrowed from a third to give to a fourth and so on until by some miracle a hundred dollars arrived in the mail from an American relative and you were able to clear debts. It was a way of life. There were no banks to lend you money on your signature or credit unions or savings and loans. Neighbors relied on each other. Kindness got each of us through difficult spots.

I came from a large family. There was my father, Mendel, an intelligent, bright, learned man who spent as much time with his studies as he did working and sleeping. Every night Father got into bed with a Talmudic book. He read until his eyeglasses fell off, the book slipped from his hand, and he was asleep. There was my mother, Sara, who read from the

Bible to my sisters, Deena and Goldie, as they did their daily chores.

Besides Tuli, I had three other brothers. There was Lipes, whom I remember little of, since he was married and out of the house before I finished elementary school. The others were Joseph and Pincus.

I lived with my family until I was thirteen. Then for three years I went to Yeshiva in another town, as was often the custom.

When I returned to Kisvárda at sixteen, I had to enter the national guard. All boys of that age were required to do so. It entailed weekend training in discipline and weaponry. It was there that I was made especially aware that, being Jewish, I was something other than Hungarian.

I always had been aware of the danger of being Jewish. When I was nine, the Jews of Kisvárda held an all-night vigil, praying that Hitler would not take over Germany. When I was a child growing up, my father had taught me not to get into arguments. The only way to avoid getting your head bashed in was to avoid arguments. If there was a bully up ahead, cross the street.

In the national guard it was made all the clearer that we were different. After four hours of maneuvering with everyone else, the Jewish boys were given extra chores. I resented it and got into fights over it. The field commander, who was all of twenty-four or twenty-five, would have none of it. He had the final say and he wanted the Jews to know they weren't as good as the other boys. As punishment I was locked in a dark closet on Sundays until I learned to keep my mouth shut.

There was a group of my Jewish friends, including Majsi,

Phillip, Frankel, and Kakas, who would meet in regularly in the parks. We were political and tried to keep in touch with the world by speaking with people who traveled a lot, by reading the papers, and by listening to the BBC radio broadcasts.

We knew that Hitler spelled bad times ahead for the European Jews. We would try to figure out something we could do besides wait to fall at the mercy of this Hitler. We wanted to go to Romania and then Palestine, to save as many people as possible.

I was always having arguments about this with my father. He saw no need for preparations. We were God-fearing people who performed properly in God's eyes. God had saved the Jews in the past and he could save them again.

Besides, Father believed that God had already allotted to you what was coming to you. There was no use fighting it.

"But Father," I would say, "that's not enough. We should get ready to fight back and not wait for some miracle. It might not come this time."

Came 1939, Hitler invaded Poland, and it was really too late for us to leave anyway.

As we listened to the BBC reports, in basements, in storerooms, on rooftops, there was no report of what was really going on, that a particular people, the Jews, were in a particular trouble. We heard some reports from Poland that Jewish families were being displaced, businesses confiscated, farms taken away, but we had no idea this was in prelude to being rounded up in camps and being killed.

If the Western world had given us some warning of the total liquidation of the Jewish people in all countries occupied by the Germans, we surely would not have waited peacefully, arms folded, to be pushed into the boxcars and carried off to the gas chambers.

Who could conceive that someone like Mr. Wilner, the freight man, was considered an enemy of the Third Reich? Mr. Wilner, who while hauling freight from the railroad station would never fail to say his morning and evening prayers. He could barely feed his horse, much less his children, who were all sent off to learn a trade when they turned thirteen.

How could Béla, the tavern owner, be anyone's enemy? And yet, in 1941, Nazi sympathizers came in and broke everything in his tavern and house, pulled his beard out of his face, broke his leg, beat his children, and abused his daughters.

I would say to my father, "Here was a man with religious fervor. He did nothing but study around the clock while his children took turns taking care of the tavern. Why didn't God use any of his miracles then?"

"You're talking like an *epikorot* [unbeliever]," Father would say, and that would end the discussion.

Some Polish Jews did escape the camps, bringing tales of atrocities with them, but no one had any idea of the extent of the killing machinery that Germany had set up, that we were in the middle of a holocaust. The true ingenuity and accomplishment of the Germans was shown in the skill and expertise with which they were able to cover up their crimes.

My family, like other Jews in Hungary, carried on as the war progressed, putting up with the restrictions and hardships placed on us, wondering what would come next.

The "next" came for me at the end of 1943. I turned twenty on December 19. By law, all twenty-year-old Hungarian men had to serve full-time in the army.

My orders to join a company did not come for several months. On Sunday, April 16, 1944, after saying goodbye to my parents, my unmarried sister, my married, pregnant sister and her husband, my brothers, the wives of the three that were married, and my six nieces and nephews, I left.

There were 220 in my company. We were transported to a camp two hundred kilometers away. There a Hungarian officer, a middle-aged former customs man named Szalay Geza, lectured us on our duties and what to expect. As Jews we could not bear arms, but we were still part of the army, and we would perform necessary work duties for the army. Geza promised that if we worked faithfully and diligently, no harm would come to us.

Most of the men would be repairing railroad tracks. Some few were needed for other tasks. We were asked if any specialists were among us—shoemakers, tailors, mechanics,

Harry in the labor camp (in the dark coat). The officer who helped him is seated in the back.

doctors, pharmacists. I volunteered that my specialty was horses. My family had two that I cared for, so I figured this was enough qualification. Someone had to drive horses and wagons with supplies and take officers around. I had a hunch that being wagoneer would pay off by putting me in an advantageous position.

It did. For one thing, I was more in touch with Geza than the others. He was a good man who took a liking to me.

"I'm going to keep you all informed about your exact status," he told me once. "If the Germans make any move to take you out of the country, where it will be more dangerous for you, I will give you advance warning. Then you can take the proper action."

Two week later, Geza selected me to accompany him back to Kisvárda. During the fourteen days I had been gone a terrible transformation had occurred. Hundreds and hundreds of Jews from nearby villages, along with the thousands of Jews of Kisvárda, had been pushed into one section of town. My family was in there somewhere, and I had to see them.

Geza pleaded that I be allowed to find and visit them. I entered the ghetto a privileged individual, under protection of the Hungarian army, with permission to visit for one hour.

My family, all thirteen of them, were in an apartment that had one bedroom, a kitchen, and a pantry, nothing more. They were frightened and hungry.

I decided to use my privilege and leave the ghetto to buy them food. I smuggled two baskets back. Not much, but enough for their immediate survival.

My parents were terrified for me. They said I was playing with my life, risking it for them.

"That's the way I felt. I did it. Now don't worry."

I tried to talk my brothers into going with me. It would ease the crowding, and I was sure Geza would let them "join" our company. They refused to leave the others. Then I would stay too.

It was too dangerous, my parents argued. I would be no use in the ghetto. Go back to the army. They would see me later, when this all passed.

I returned to my troop working on the railroad in Kosica. They were reinforcing tracks, fixing loose stones, mending crossbars.

I took food to the workers each day. More and more frequently we were seeing trains coming through filled with people, Jews, being taken to Poland.

It was June, and it was hot. The trains were often shunted off to side tracks as express trains and military transports came through. There the people would wait, locked in their boxes, suffocating in the sun with no water.

I carried two collapsible canvas bags to water my horses. "Let me give some water to those poor people," I begged the officers. The dirge-like moaning in the cars was heartrending. I got permission.

The people begged me for news. What was going to happen to them? Where were they going? I felt like an idiot. All I knew was that they were heading toward Poland.

I made up my mind then that no one would put me into a boxcar and lock the door, without my knowing what was the last stop. My fate would be no train ride.

The train guards claimed the people were going to camps in the east, that the men would be separated from the women and children and only they would be made to work. All would be well. I knew that was a lie, the biggest lie, and I wasn't going to fall for it.

We worked in Kosica until August. Then the trains stopped coming. We were ordered to move out.

We went west, to four miles from Budapest on the Danube River. There the company was put to work repairing roads.

I was sent two or three times a week into the city to get supplies at a refrigerated warehouse.

On one of those trips I heard my name being called. I looked around and at first couldn't figure out where the "Harry! Harry!" was coming from. Then I saw, but I couldn't believe it. It was Jossi Klein, a lifelong friend from Kisvárda. He was unloading coal from a boxcar.

Klein had been working around Budapest for a while, he told me. He had come in contact with an organized, underground movement that was, among other things, supplying people with Aryan papers and German documents. It seemed that the only escape was with false papers. I made note of their hideouts. On my next supply run, I made a little side trip. I made several more after that. At the right time I would know where to go.

That day came on October 15, 1944. The sham of an independent Hungary was crumbling. Another pro-German government had been installed, and the collaborators were handing the country over to Hitler completely.

Geza called me aside. "It's all over," he said. "The moderates are gone. Things have gotten too dangerous. Make your move."

I took my wagon and horses into Budapest. I didn't want to, but I had to abandon them. I went to join the underground.

The resistance had been growing rapidly as army deserters joined forces with Jews. The group I got myself into set up headquarters in a film factory that had been abandoned by the national film industry.

There were about sixty of us. We set up the place as if it were a legitimate military office. We had people working at desks during the day, watchmen at night. The rest of us hid in the warehouse.

We ventured out dressed as soldiers, with stolen documents and vehicles. By all appearances we were legitimate.

But we did the work of missionaries. We "liberated" food warehouses and distributed the food. We took food to those in hiding. We sabotaged bridges and railroad crossings and blew up strategic buildings.

We also patrolled at night, looking for German collaborators who might be harassing distressed people. It happened all the time. Collaborators stopped people on the street, examined documents, and if they were the least bit suspicious, took them to the Danube, where they were shot—if they didn't shoot them right on the spot.

We took care of those collaborators.

We operated for two months. During that time I got some fake Swiss in-transit papers stating that I was a Swiss citizen on my way to South America. They were insurance.

One Friday, we got word from sympathizers at downtown army headquarters that suspicious questions were being asked. Exactly who was out at the film warehouse? Which outfit? What were they doing?

We knew the time had come. It was decided that on Sunday we would break through German lines and make our way to the Russians, who were only a half hour from the city.

It was that or disperse and flee. We chose to fight with the Allies.

It wasn't to be. Saturday night one of the watchmen ran to where we were in the warehouse. There were about a dozen German SS and Hungarian collaborators outside. They wanted in. They didn't believe the watchmen were the only ones there.

We held a hurried conference. There would be no surrender. We would wait until the Germans stormed the door; then we would fight and run.

I saw at least six or seven German SS hit. I didn't know how many of our people fell. I took to the fields and ran back to the center of Budapest, throwing away my leather coat, all evidence of the military, and my weapons—four grenades, bullets, a gun. I kept my other pistol, which I stuck into my waistband.

I would have to rely on my insurance, the Swiss documents.

I was sweating, and not from heat, as I walked along Vadasz Street to the makeshift Swiss consulate. There had been so many asking for asylum that the consulate had left its former building for a larger one. There were German SS soldiers everywhere, more than I had seen before. I don't know what I would have done had I known that they were there keeping surveillance on the consulate, ready to stop anyone trying to enter.

It was a sheer miracle I made it to the consulate gate without being stopped. A guard opened the gate a crack and asked what I wanted.

"I am here with a visa in my pocket. I would like to ask for asylum because of the unstable condition in the city. I would rather like to wait out these difficult times inside the consulate."

He started to shut the gate, explaining he couldn't let me in without checking first.

I stuck my foot in the door and pulled out the gun. "Let me in or I'll let you have it."

He stepped aside and I was inside. In the courtyard I was relieved, but I had not been admitted to the building. The guard went off to find certain people who knew me. They had given me the papers. At last I was vouched for.

I had to give up the gun before being taken to a cavernous basement filled with other scared men and women, boys and girls.

So we remained. The basement became more crowded every day. The Swiss were giving more and more people asylum. A Swedish diplomat was planting his country's flag on building after building, declaring them neutral territory, and then filling them with people carrying Swedish passports he had printed himself.

Finally the Swiss took over the building next to the one I was in. It had been the headquarters of the Hungarian national soccer organization, and it had six stories. During bombing raids people crowded down into its basement for protection.

I stayed above. I didn't care about bombs or dying from hunger or exhaustion. What mattered to me was that I not fall into German hands to be massacred by them. Anyone could die from a bomb or an accident or stepping on a grenade. I would not die because I had been singled out as a Jew. That I refused to do.

During one raid, I was on the third floor with a couple of others, even though the bombs were very close. Suddenly there was a tremendous thud that kept on sounding, tearing away at the building. We looked up, and above our heads was the tip of an enormous bomb. It had fallen through three floors without exploding. If it had, one thousand people would have been killed.

February 14, 1945, the Russians took Budapest.

It meant no liberation for me. I was taken with many others from the consulate building into a work crew that was herded across the frozen Danube to dismantle unexploded bombs. We were going to be treated as conquered Hungarians—papers to the contrary or no—and would be put to work doing chores the Russians didn't care to do themselves.

I was with the crew for twelve hours.

That night we were being marched to a schoolhouse to spend the night before beginning more work in the morning. I left the line and escaped.

That was the last time I was ever in captivity.

I waited for two years in Kisvárda. I waited for someone in my immediate family to come back. No one did.

I found one cousin who had escaped death by diving into the icy Danube when he had been lined up alongside it, with hundreds of others, to be shot. He swam underwater as far as he could, then swam farther. A couple of miles downriver, he pulled himself out, almost dead from frostbite and exposure, and knocked on the first door he came to. There was no reason those people had to take him in. They did, and my cousin lived.

The one person who did come back was my brother-in-law Tuli. He had been married to Deena; he was the pious son-in-law my father so wanted. He and my four brothers,

Lipe, Jossi, Pinchas, and Naphtali, had been sent to work in a coal mine. There Tuli alone survived. There he had become a leader and survived by getting extra pieces of bread. He had seen my brothers, passed out from malnutrition, with swollen legs and bellies, sent to the "recuperation rooms," rooms no one ever came out of alive.

Mother, pregnant Deena, Goldie (she who so feared death —what must have been her thoughts in the cattle car, in the gas chamber?), and Father were sent to no work camps. They were taken immediately from the trains to death.

Hungary was no longer a place for me to live.

Out of four thousand Jews in Kisvárda, several hundred remained alive. Why did so, so many of them walk into those cattle wagons, into those gas chambers, or stand passively on the banks of the Danube to be shot? Why did we sit like ducks and not fight back? Was it only because of that blind belief in miracles and our lot?

People today don't wait like sitting ducks. Cubans don't like the regime? They crowd on boats and get away. South Koreans don't like martial law? They riot in protest. Up until that last moment of life, did my father still believe God would save him?

The Sabras, the Israeli-born Jews, are embarrassed by the passivity that allowed us to be ground up in the German killing machines like so much meat.

There are no Jews left today in Kisvárda, only tombstones. The marvelously constructed temple, which once seated the entire Jewish community, now stands empty.

I could no longer live in Hungary. There was nothing left for me there.

I made my way to France and waited one year for a visa.

On December 19, 1949, my twenty-sixth birthday, I arrived in the United States, alone.

A few weeks later, at Purim, a stranger in the synagogue told me he had a sister.

Four months later, on May 28, I married that sister and was no longer alone.

34

In most ways, it has been a good and fulfilling thirty years.

At first, like so many young couples, we had to struggle financially.

Harry got himself into the garment industry quite by accident. Shortly after he arrived in the United States, he took the subway from Brooklyn to the Bronx. On the ride he got into a conversation with a stranger. By the time they reached Harry's station, the stranger had told Harry to drop by his factory on Monday. The man knew that his boss needed workers. It was a dress plant, and Harry got the job.

After we were married, Harry worked hard, sometimes at two jobs, to keep us under a roof, with money for food. We lived in a little apartment on the top floor, in Brooklyn. It was there that we brought home beautiful Cornelia Colette, who was born on October 7, 1951. We named her after my mother. In 1954, redheaded Mitchell was born.

We saved every penny we could, because Harry would never be content to be an employee. He was to be a boss. The year Mitchell was born we had enough so that Harry could start a tucking-and-stitching business with a friend.

The business grew and with it our income. We were at

last able to afford the American dream—a mortgage on a house on Long Island.

Then disaster. Our factory burned down, and only a few of the machines were saved. We went right back into business. Ends had to be met.

Icu and Margaret had got married by this time. And Miklos had come to the United States also, to marry and live in Brooklyn. Many of my Taverny friends were in the New York area, as was some of Harry's friends from Kisvárda. One of them, Sam Green, was not. He had moved to Greenville, South Carolina, where he was managing a ladies'-clothing plant.

One week in the late spring of 1959, we drove down to visit him and to get some idea what life was like in the South.

While we were there, Sam suggested we take a look at an old clothing factory for sale, not far away, in Asheville, North Carolina. The ride to Asheville, through the watershed and into the dramatic green mountains, impressed me greatly. It vaguely reminded me of Tolcsva. What is more, everyone was so friendly, although they had trouble understanding my Hungarian-Brooklyn accent and I had trouble with their drawl.

Harry and I decided to move to Asheville.

With the move came a new set of financial worries—suppliers going bankrupt and leaving us without orders; having to look for others to subcontract for. Little by little we found more business, started doing better, doing well. Today we have sixty people working in our factory producing clothes under the label of The Traveler by Connie, and we have three retail outlets.

Harry designed and had built a beautiful contemporary house for us in the hills, large and comfortable, big enough

My four wonderful children, several years ago. From left, Connie, Mitchell, Vivian, and Michael.

to accommodate Vivian, who was born on Christmas Eve, 1960.

I'll never forget the moment when the nurse brought her in, wrapped in a red and green stocking, hand-sewn, with jingle bells on it. She proclaimed, "Here she is, Mr. and Mrs. Lerner, your Christmas gift from Santa!" Harry replied, "It's Chanukah, dahling, Chanukah."

Then, in 1969, Joseph was born, redheaded like his brother.

We grew to like the small-town, sylvan atmosphere of Asheville, its only drawback being its distance from our friends and relatives.

Our children grew to give us much pleasure and many reasons to have pride in them.

Mitchell today is finishing up his master's at York University in Toronto and probably will go on to law school.

Vivian, who is as beautiful as her sister, is also at the University of Toronto and may become an actress.

Joseph is at home, but time is slipping away so quickly; it won't be long before he's off on his own also.

Connie is married to a son of two survivors, and now has three children of her own. (In one of life's incredible coincidences, her mother-in-law was among those jaundice-yellow girls who joined out *Lager* in Leipzig after their camp was bombed.)

Both Connie and Vivian are beauty-contest winners. Vivian was first runner up in the Miss North Carolina–Miss USA pageant., Connie made it to Atlantic City as Miss North Carolina, the year Phyllis George became Miss America.

For her talent selection my beautiful daughter played the "Revolutionary Etude," by Chopin, because that's what the Poles played over and over on the radio in defiance of Hitler when he invaded in 1939. She could have played "The

Connie as Miss North Carolina.

Sound of Music" or "Singing in the Rain," but she was too honest for that.

Her honesty quite astounded the press during her reign as Miss North Carolina. They were used to the standard simpering Southern belle, not the daughter of Holocaust survivors quite open and willing to discuss the Holocaust. Being Miss North Carolina is big stuff in the state. She's practically second to the governor. The day after Connie won, I remember the headlines and stories that ran throughout the state. "The daughter of Jewish immigrants persecuted in World War II, Miss Lerner retains much of their sense of the tangibility of civil liberties and peace."

35

In 1965 my friends from Buchenwald and Taverny had a reunion.

We met Judith at the airport, bouquets in hand.

"I recognize every one of you. And you, Mr. Margulies—you are here too!"

No one had changed for her. "It is the same family. The years have gone, but our friendship has remained."

The big formal dinner we had was both solemn and lively, with emotions laid out in the open.

One speaker was particularly moving. "We have come together here tonight, not only to celebrate the victory of our survival, but to remember all those who are not here with us. Here it is twenty years since we were fighting, twenty years since we swam over the shore. Those twenty years were pretty difficult to live. We never had time to stop and think of parents, of our brothers, of our sisters, of our families, of the many people from our villages and town who are not here. Therefore, we have gathered together tonight to think of them. Let us get up and observe a minute of silence and say *Kaddish* * for them."

* Kaddish: the Jewish prayer for the dead.

My brother Icu's gravestone.

It was a night of many memories.

In 1965, shortly after the reunion, I received a call from Brooklyn.

Icu was in the hospital undergoing extensive tests. I took the next flight from Asheville.

He had a malignant tumor on the right side of his brain. We kept the knowledge from him for a while. But his condition got worse. His speech was affected. He had always been a superb speaker, this highly intelligent, compassionate, and warm scholar of the Talmud. And now it was gone.

Icu, with his goodness and strong character, was to my mind never an ordinary person. He was highly respected by his friends and in the community. It was hard to believe that this was to be the end of such a beautiful human being.

It is hard to conceive what he went through in those last weeks of his life. I visited him regularly. He stared at me with his beautiful eyes, the only way he could communicate, since words could no longer come from his mouth. He used to tell me, long ago, how life was unimportant, how it was only a preparation for the life hereafter, how only the shell suffers by death.

He was a pious and true person. A good husband and father of four.

We buried him in Israel.

Now there are no more telephone calls with a friendly voice at the other end asking, *"Wus machst du?"* (How are you?)

He was the first of the Taverny boys to die.

36

I have not forgotten, nor do I try. I have gone back to Auschwitz. I have seen it turned into a tourist attraction, where families picnic within it. I visited the grave of my father. I have gone to my husband's birthplace in Kisvárda, to the remains and monuments of other camps, where the fourteen million were destroyed.

I suffer the memories and the reminders.

Why do I return to where our families were broken up and killed? Back to places where smiles were frozen and erased from even those who survived?

I go back for one more look, one more experience, to fulfill my responsibility as a survivor. I feel the weight of the importance to remember and to tell the story, my story.

I had a dream.

I dreamed I was in Aunt Hani's house in Tolcsva, a house I have never seen in real life, since she had moved before I was born.

She was having a big celebration.

Her children were there and her grandchildren as well. There were other cousins, more distant, from America. It was a reunion in a hall decorated with red, white, and blue ribbons. The waiters wore white wigs and had blue satin jackets over their white shimmering pants.

But something was wrong. If this was a reunion, where was the rest of the family? Where was my mother, my father, Uncles Louis, Henry, Sam, and the others? Where were Ernoke and Aunt Boriska, Aunt Ilonka? If this was a family reunion, why weren't they here?

"Don't worry," Aunt Hani reassured me. "You'll be seeing them soon."

The party went on, and they didn't come.

I promised my cousins they would be meeting my wonderful father whom I used to follow like a little puppy. They, too, would hear his whistling and stories of the war. And my mother, so beautiful and good. She would be there too.

But the party went on and they didn't come.

Finally I went to Aunt Hani again. "Weren't we supposed to meet the rest of the family here?"

She took a long look at me and breathed in sorrow.

"Don't you remember? There was a Hitler. This is what's left of your family. You have no more. The rest are gone, casualties, victims, martyrs. Don't you remember at all?"

I remember everything.

These were my people, the ones I loved. There are no monuments to them, no plaques. They died for no cause, no slogans, no higher purposes. They died because they were there.

Perhaps this book will give them one minute longer in eternity, because I remember.